COLLI

HANDY ROA~~D~~ ~~ATLAS~~

BRITAIN
& IRELAND

CONTENTS

2	**Key to Map Symbols**
3-49	**Map Pages of Britain at 9 miles to 1 inch**
50-53	**Urban Area Maps at approx 4 miles to 1 inch**
50-51	London and M25
52-53	Birmingham
54-60	**Map Pages of Ireland at 16 miles to 1 inch**
61-77	**Index to Place Names in Britain**
78-79	**Index to Place Names in Ireland**

Published by Collins
An imprint of HarperCollins*Publishers*
77–85 Fulham Palace Road, Hammersmith, London W6 8JB

The HarperCollins website address is: www.**fire**and**water**.com

Copyright © HarperCollins*Publishers* Ltd 2000
Mapping © Bartholomew Ltd 1998, 1999, 2000

Collins ® is a registered trademark of HarperCollins*Publishers* Limited

Mapping generated from the Bartholomew digital databases

Bartholomew website address is: www.bartholomewmaps.com

Printed in Hong Kong   NC10720   BDD
ISBN 0 00 449068 1 paperback
ISBN 0 00 710757 9 spiral
e-mail: roadcheck@harpercollins.co.uk

KEY TO SYMBOLS

ROAD INFORMATION

under constr.
M1 = = = =
motorway

motorway tunnel

restricted access
1 ————— **2**
junction number

restricted access
service area

dual carriageway
A1
primary route

dual carriageway —— under constr.
A634 - - - - - -
'A' road

dual carriageway —— under constr.
B1246 - - - - - -
'B' road

other road

13
distance in miles

gradient

toll

OTHER TRANSPORT INFORMATION

——)——(——
railway

car ferry

airport

CITIES, TOWNS AND VILLAGES

built-up areas

settlement

Scale: approx. 9 miles to 1 inch
0   10   20 miles
0   10   20   30 km
1 : 550 000

OTHER FEATURES

international boundary

national boundary

national / regional park

forest park

woodland

beach

marsh

canal

lake , dam and river

718
△
height in metres

TOURIST INFORMATION

☆
place of interest

feet	metres
2950	900
2295	700
1640	500
985	300
657	200
328	100
0	0 land below sea level
	water

ADDITIONAL INFORMATION ON URBAN AREA MAPS PAGES 50-53

full access   limited access
30 **M4** **29**
motorway/ junctions

off road
full access   limited access
motorway services

dual   single
A48
primary route

dual   single
A30
'A' road

dual   B1403   single
'B' road

minor road

roads under construction

multi-level junction/ roundabout

road tunnel

Toll
level crossing/ toll

woodland

DUDLEY   primary route destination

Ⓗ   heliport

■ all year   information
i seasonal   centre

preserved railway

1738
battlefield

m   ancient monument

castle

historic house

ecclesiastical building

museum / art gallery

garden

country park

nature reserve

wildlife park or zoo

motor racing circuit

race course

major sports venue

theme park

golf course

(NT)   national trust property

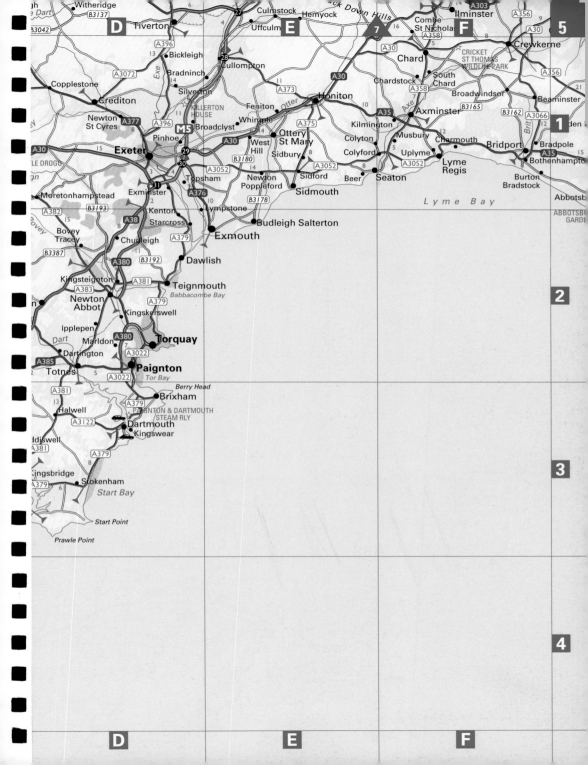

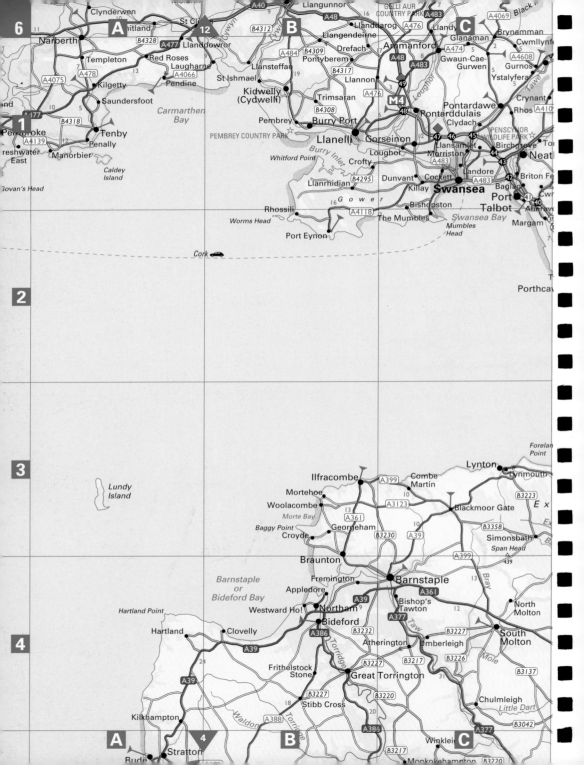

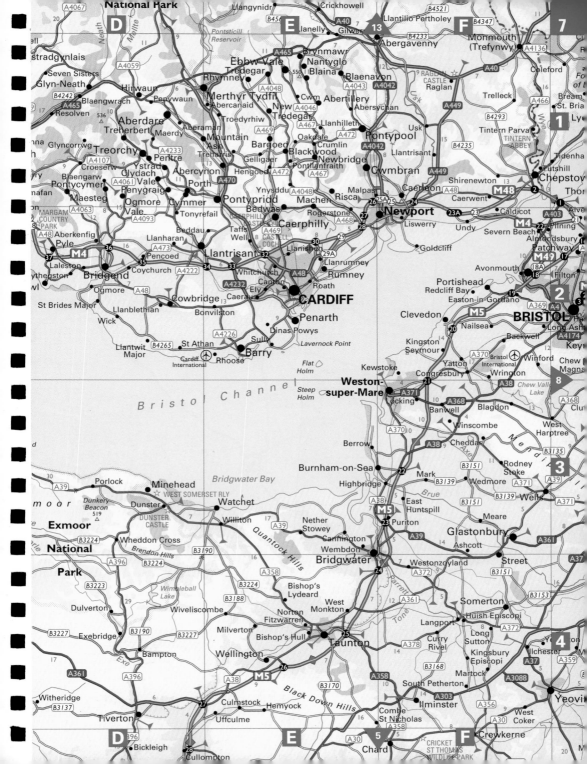

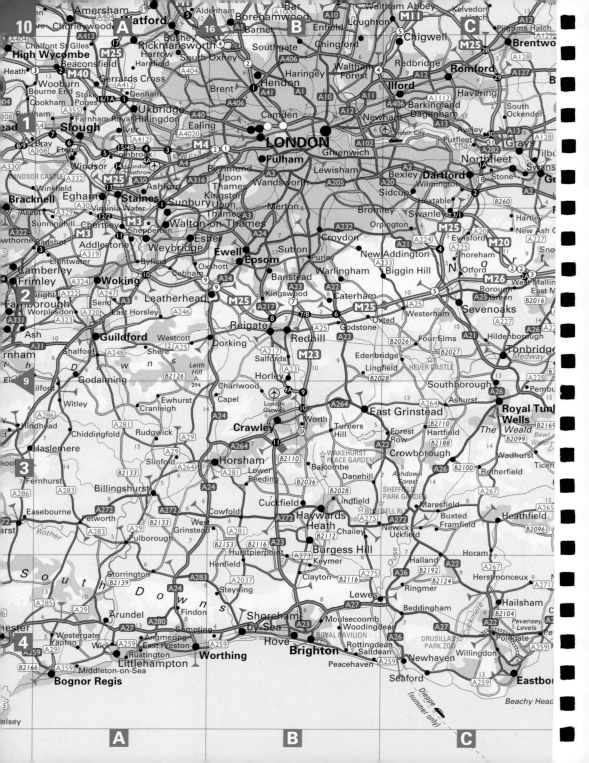

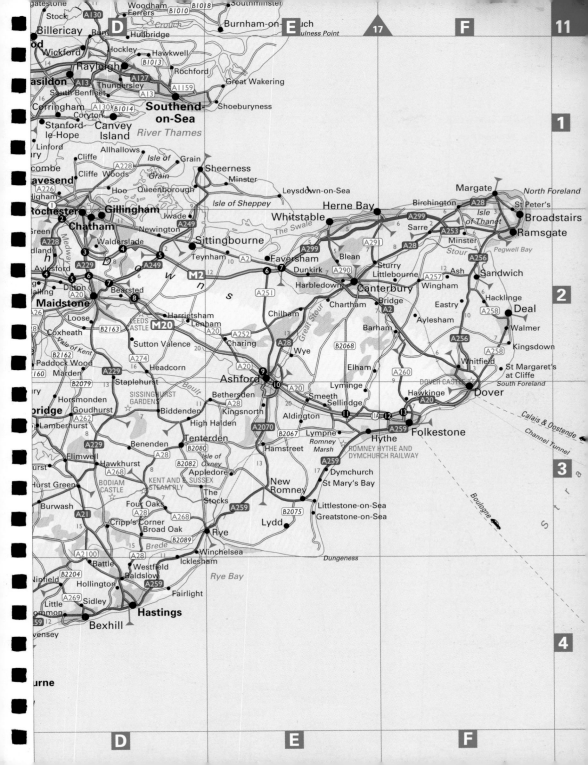

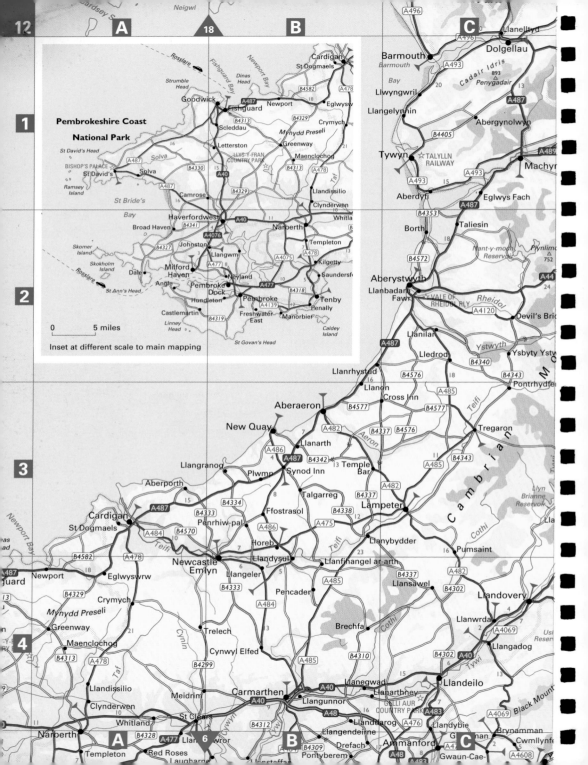

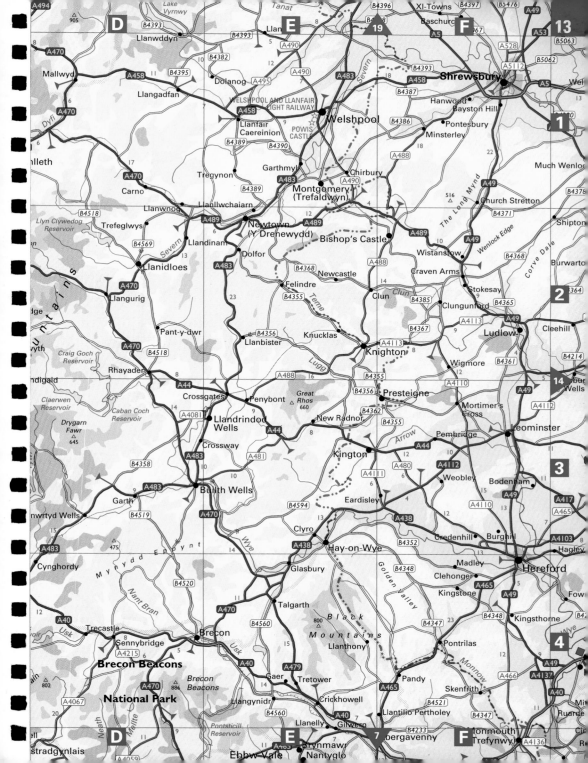

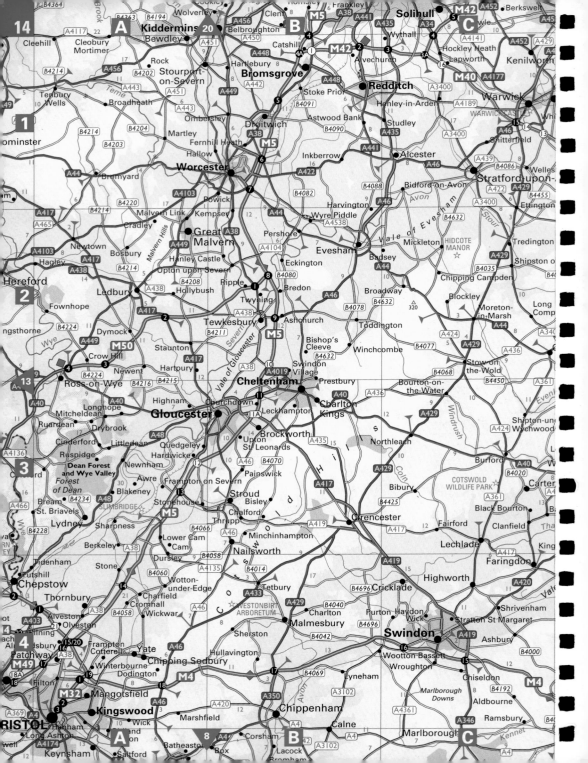

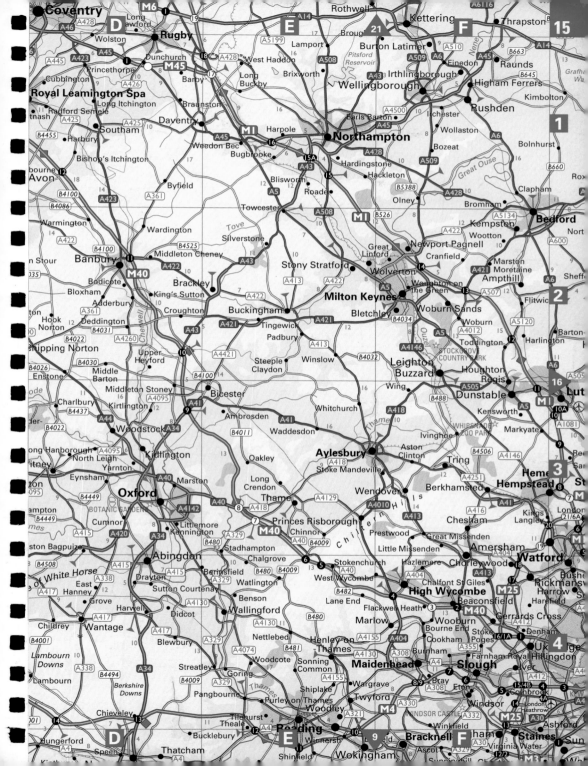

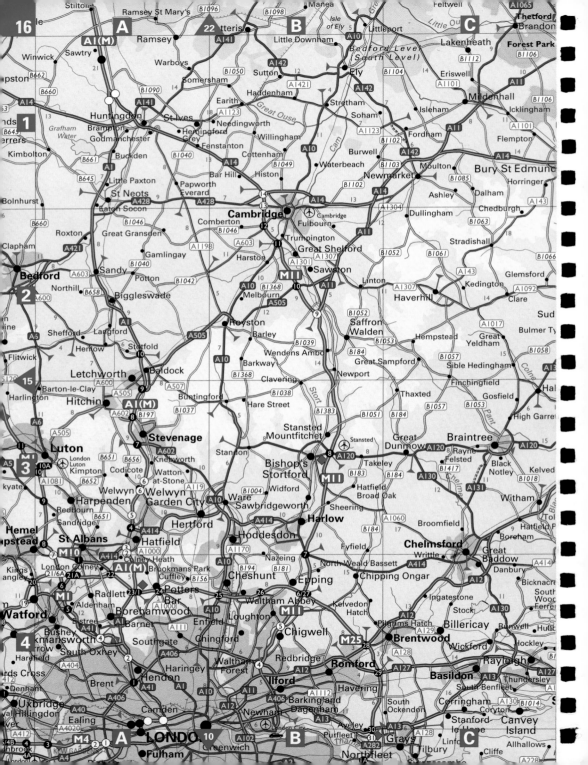

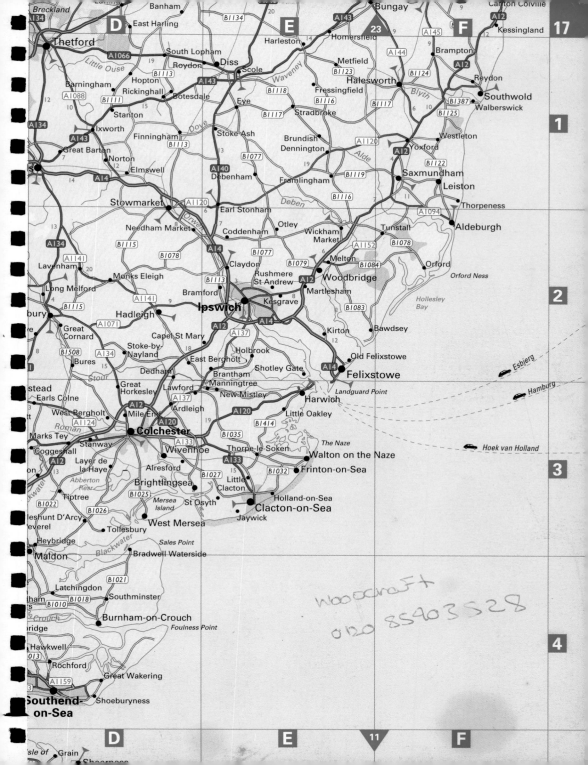

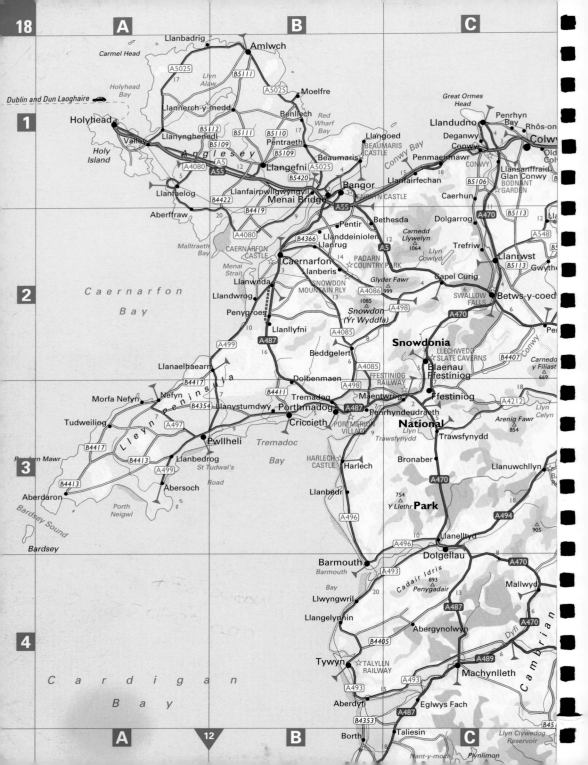

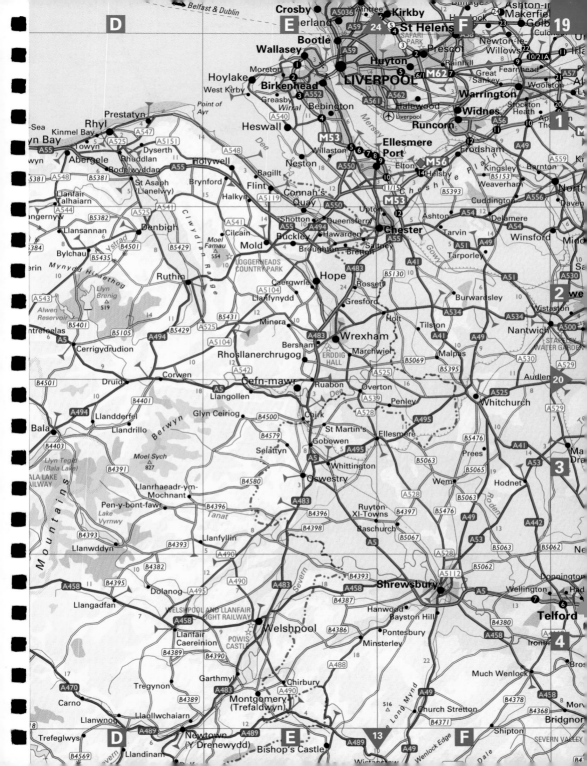

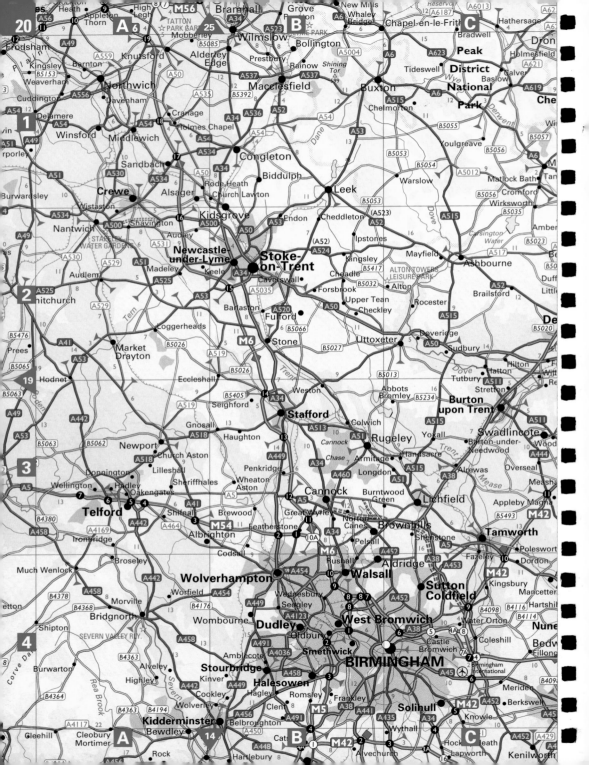

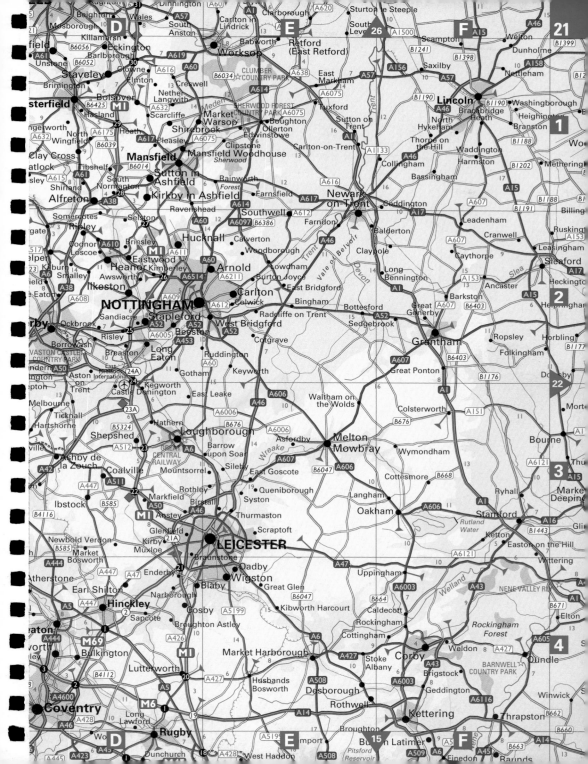

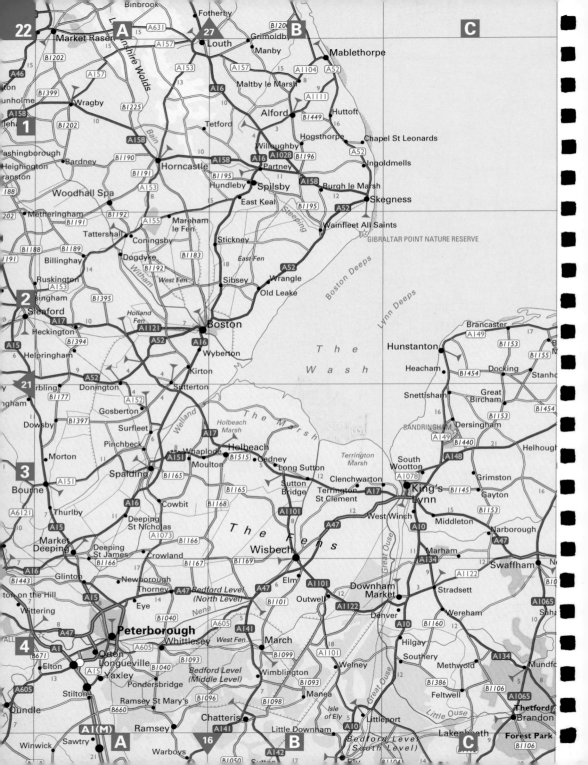

1

2

3

4

Blakeney Point

Blakeney
A149
Wells-next-the-Sea   19   Sheringham   Cromer
urnham   B1156   NORTH NORFOLK   8   B1159
Market   RAILWAY
B1105   Letheringsett   A148   Roughton   Mundesley
Holt   Thorpe Market
B1355   9   21   B1149   10   A140   A49   B1145   Happisburgh
Briston   B1354   A49   B1150
akenham   A148   Saxthorpe   BLICKLING   North   B1150
B1110   HALL   Walsham   A149
on   B1146   Guist   B1149   B354   Aylsham   BURE VALLEY   B1150   6   Stalham   B1159
A1067   Cawston   RAILWAY   Low   A49   Hickling
A1065   North Elmham   25   B1145   Reepham   A140   Bure   Street   West Somerton
14   Bawdeswell   B1149   Coltishall   Martham   Filby   Hemsby
B1145   B1147   Horstead   Hoveton   19   Broad
Swanton   Attlebridge   B1150   Horning   A1062   The   A49   Ormesby St Margaret
Morley   A1067   Horsford   Spixworth   Rackheath   Broads   A1064   Caister-on-Sea
East Dereham   Taverham   Drayton   Norwich   Salhouse   Billockby
A47   16   Sprowston   A1151   Little Plumstead   Bure
A47   A1075   A47   A1074   18   Acle   A47
ecton   Thorpe   Brundall   Great Yarmouth
77   A1075   A47   B1108   Norwich   St Andrew   Bradwell
B1135   Hethersett   A146   A143   A12
Kimberley   B1172   Cringleford   Stoke Holy Cross   17   Thurton   10   Hopton
Hingham   Gringleford   B1332   Loddon   Corton
m Toney   B1108   Wymondham   B1135   Mulbarton   Brooke   Oulton
Watton   A1075   B1077   Great Ellingham   Hales   B1136   Haddiscoe   B1074   A1117
B1108   13   Hempnall   Woodton   Lowestoft
ord   Attleborough   B1332   7   Carlton Colville
A11   B1077   B1113   Long Stratton   Beccles   A146   A12
Larling   13   Banham   A140   Bungay   A145   B1127   Kessingland
Breckland   B1134   20   A143   9   12
134   East Harling   Harleston   14   Homersfield   Bram
Thetford   South Lopham   17   A144   F
Little Ouse   6   Diss   Metfield
Roydon   Scole   B1123   A12

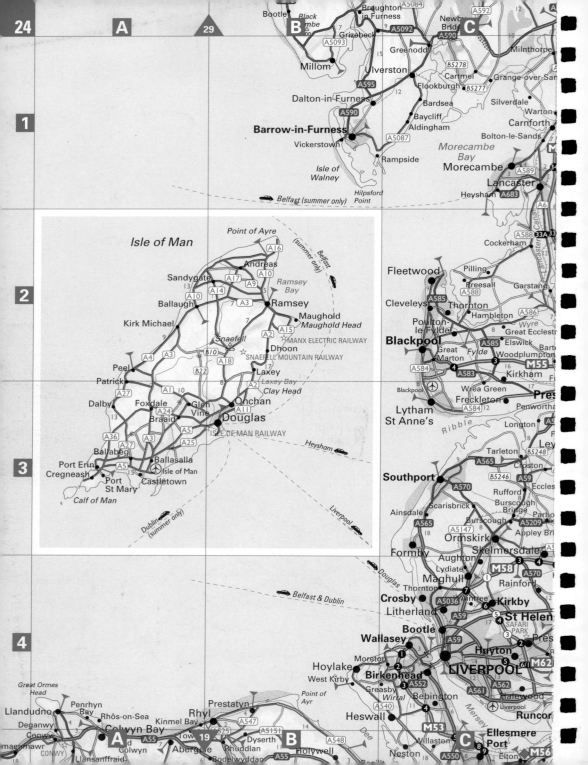

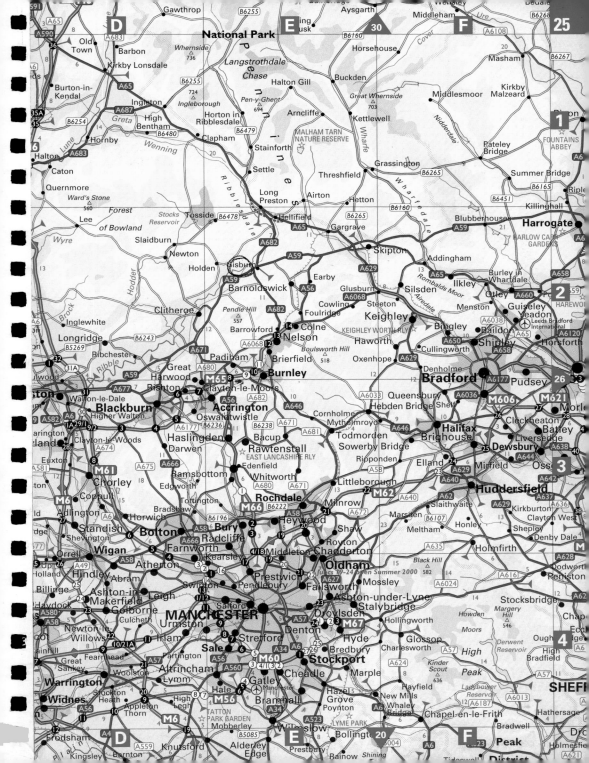

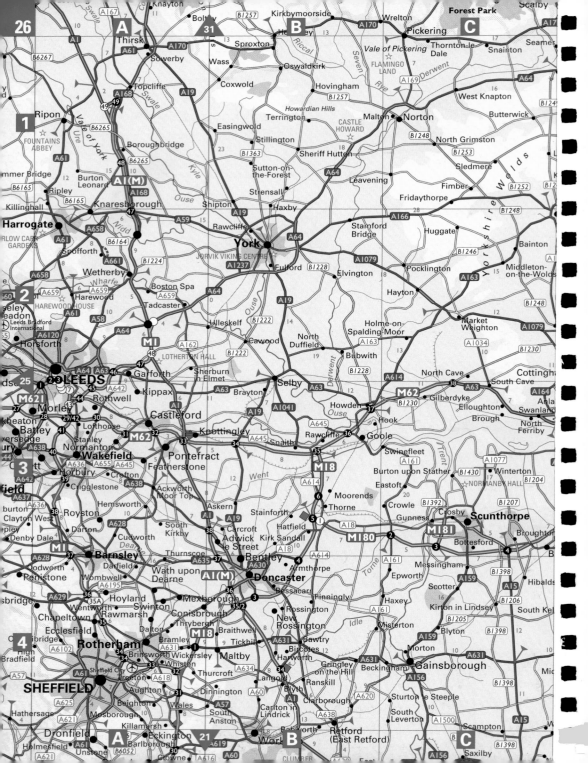

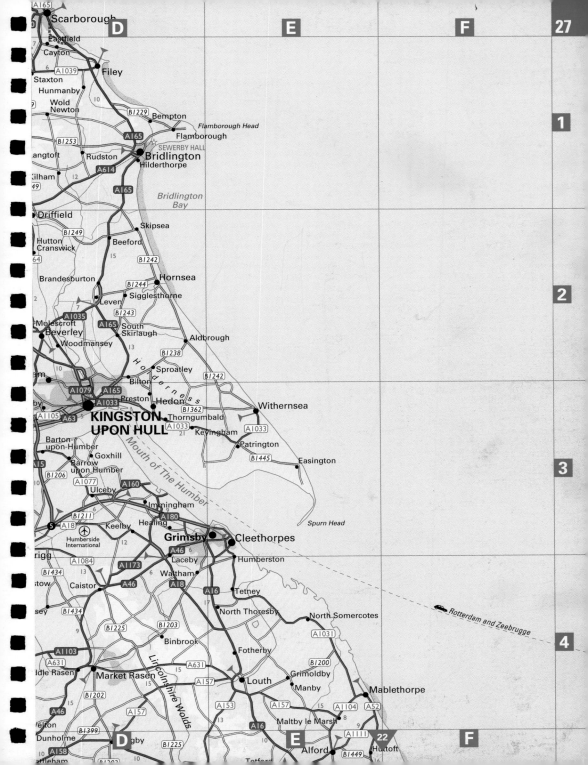

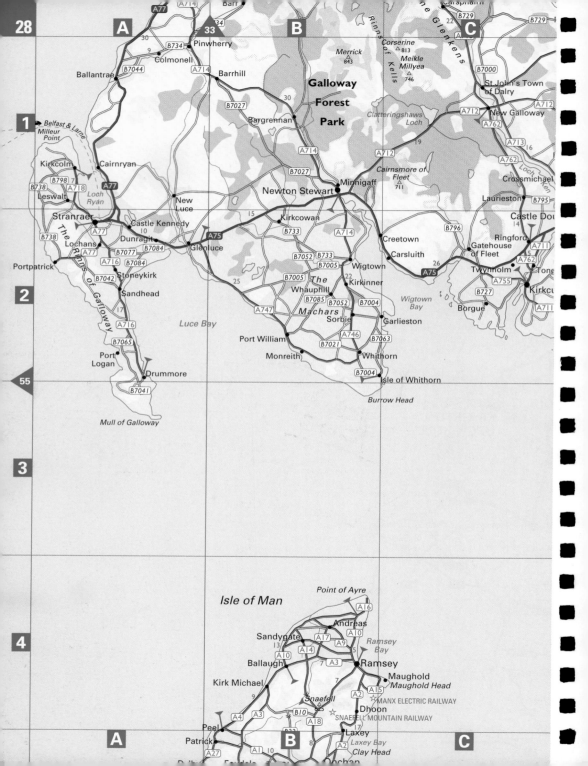

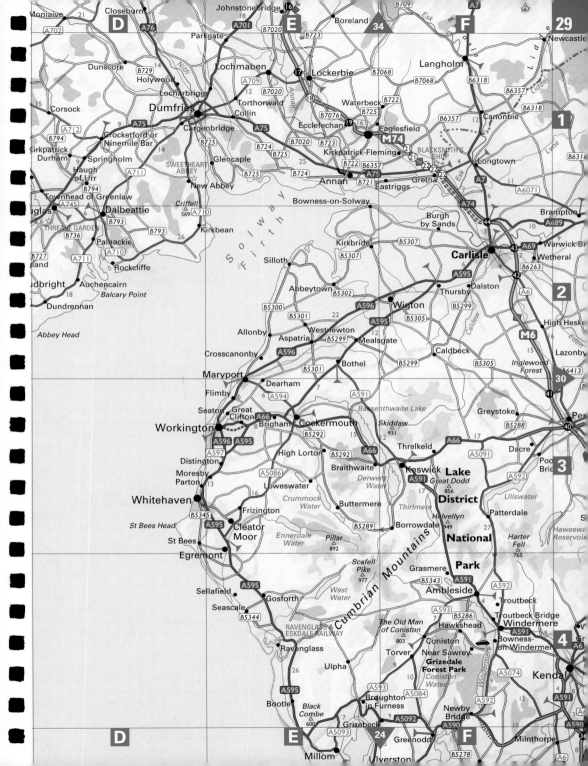

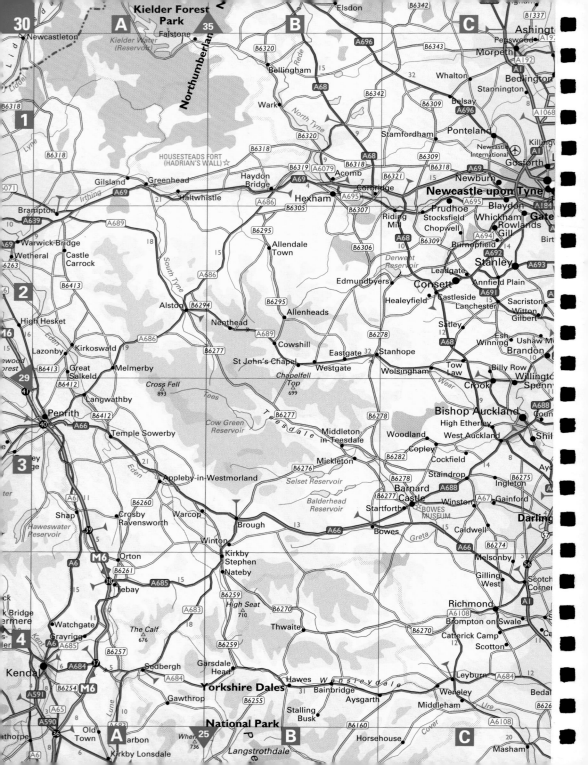

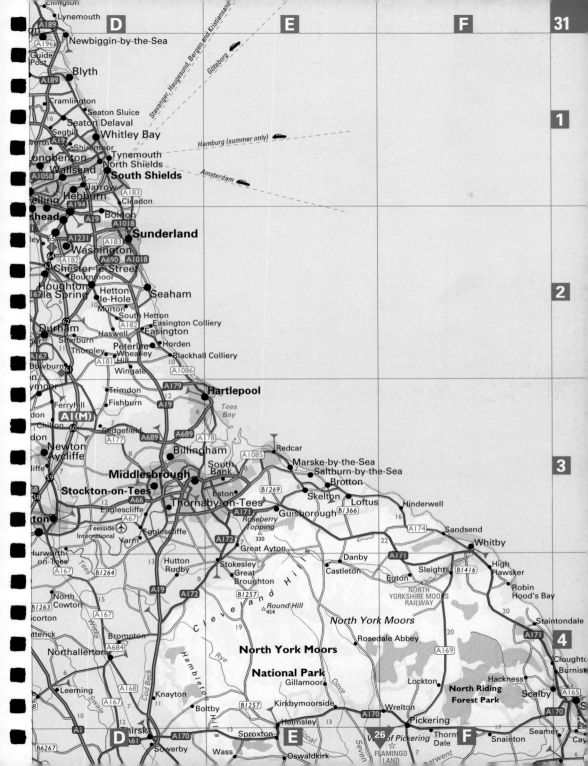

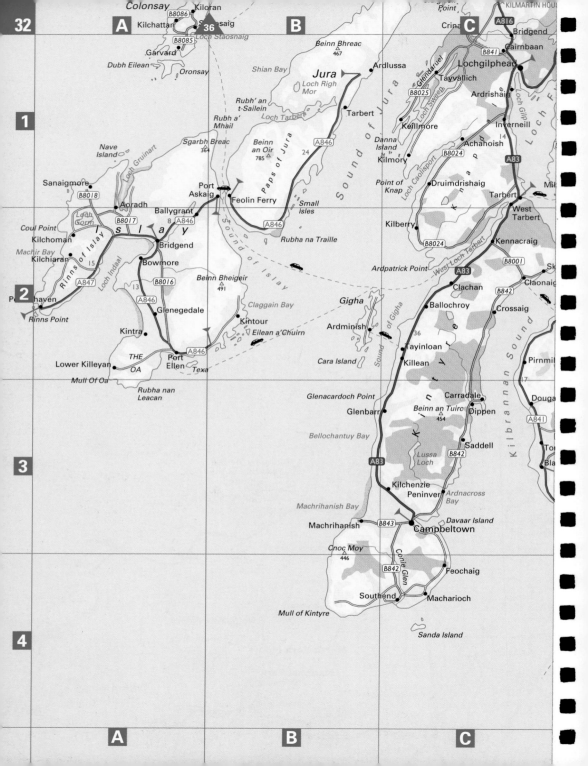

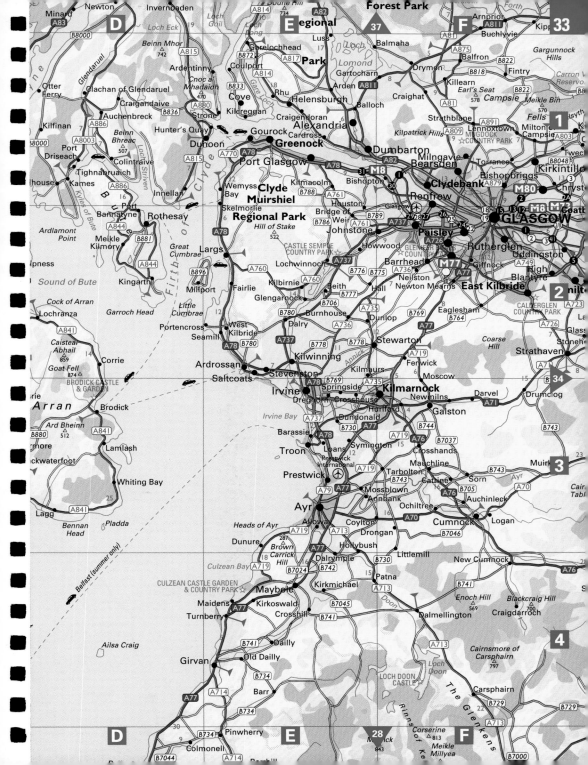

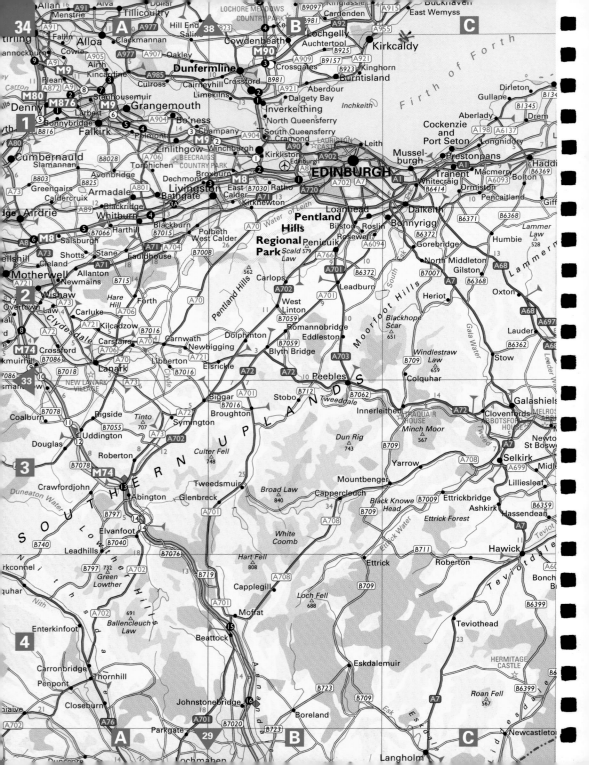

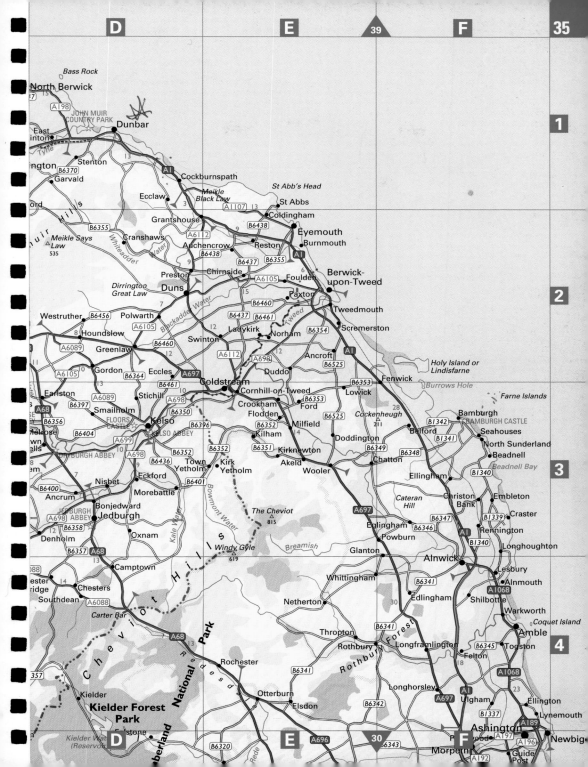

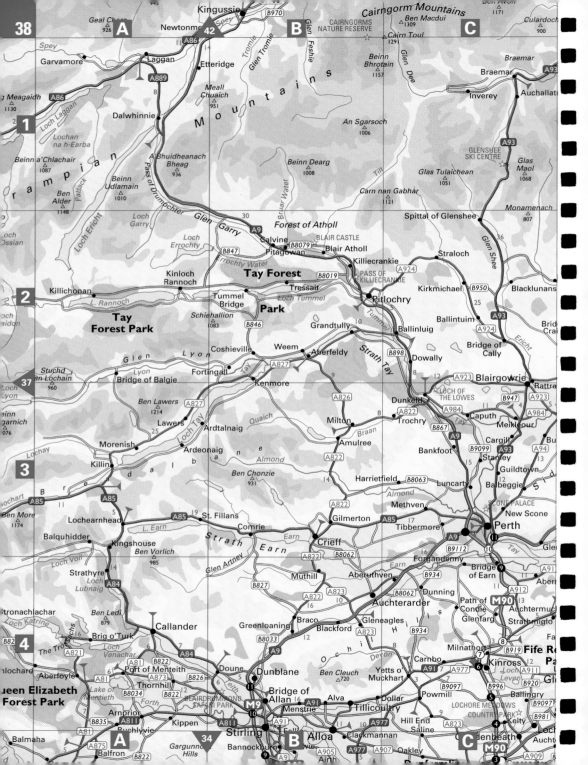

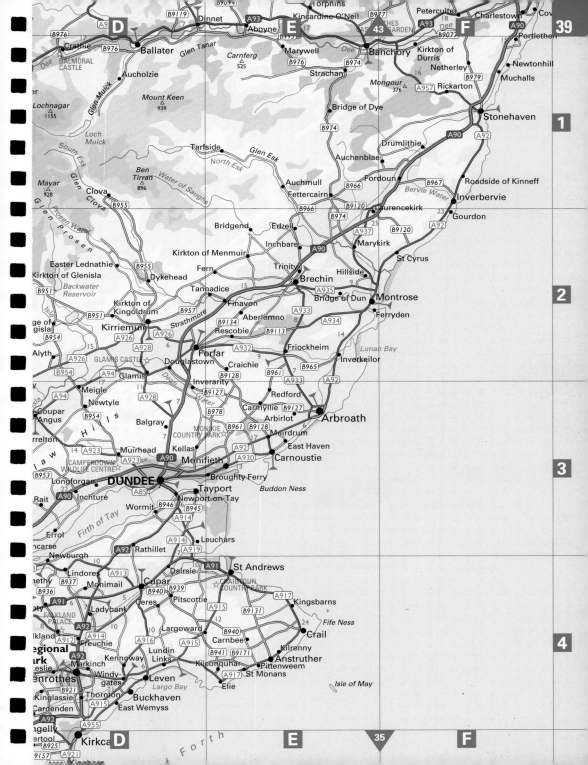

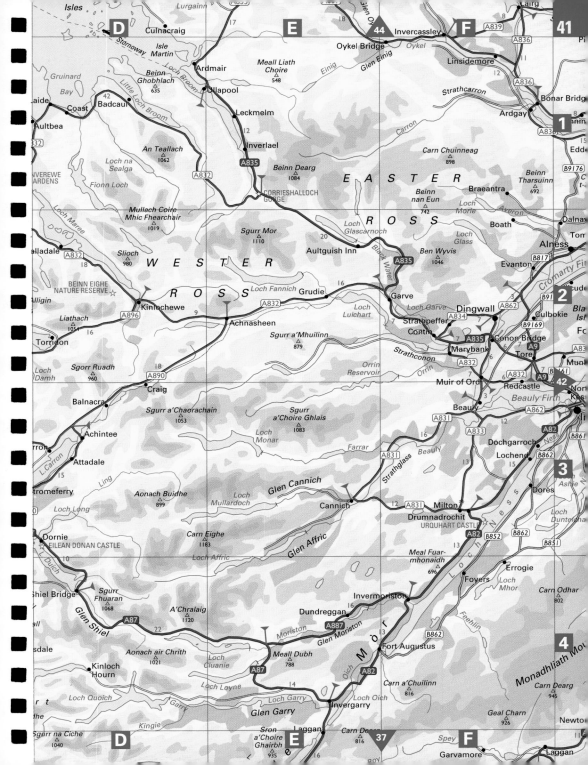

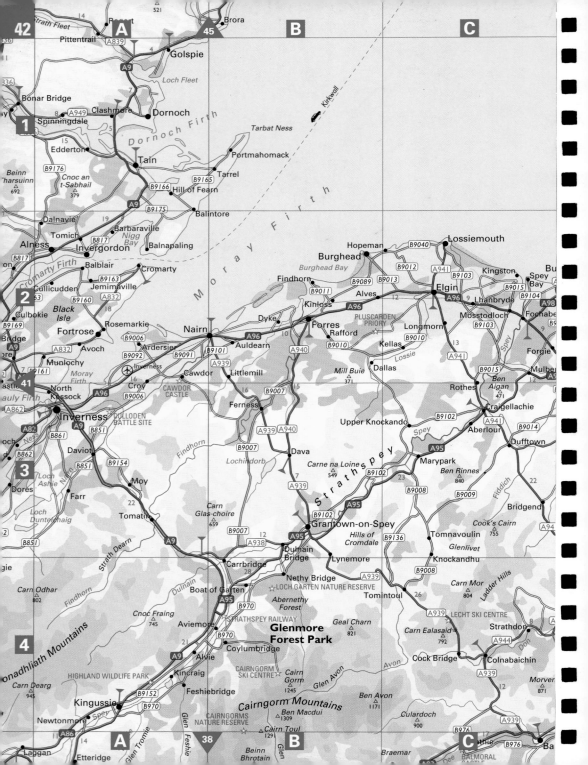

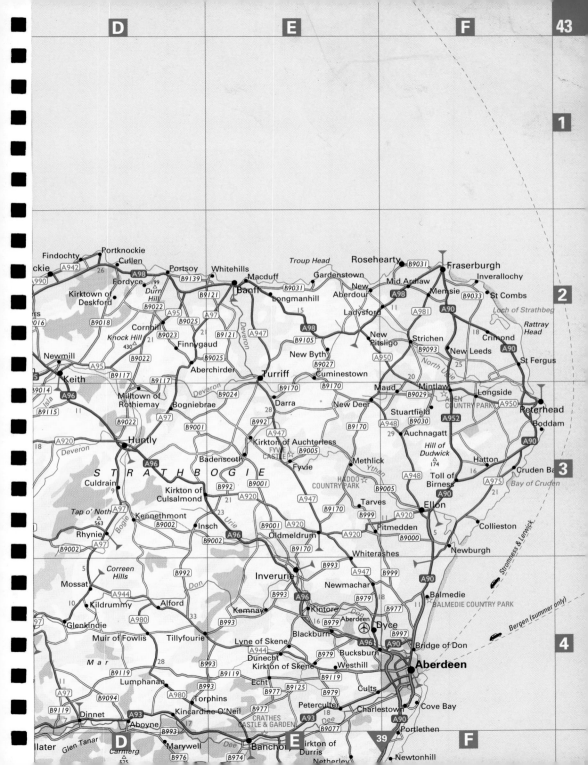

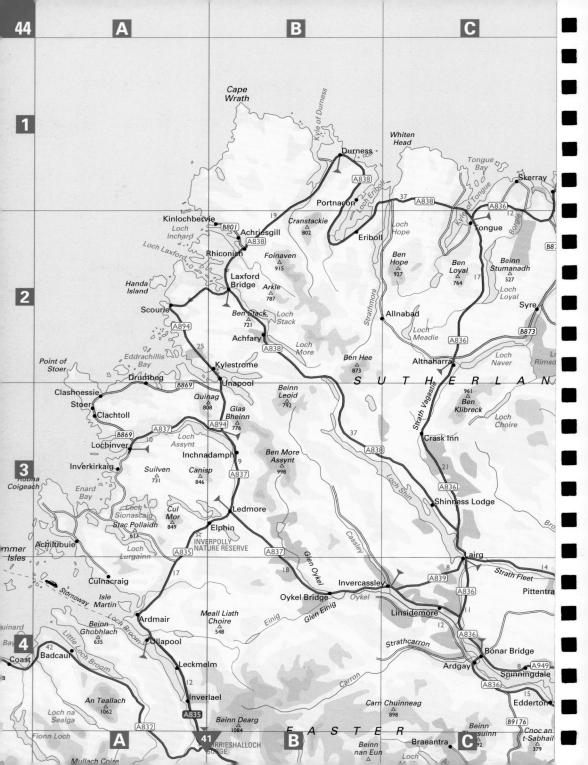

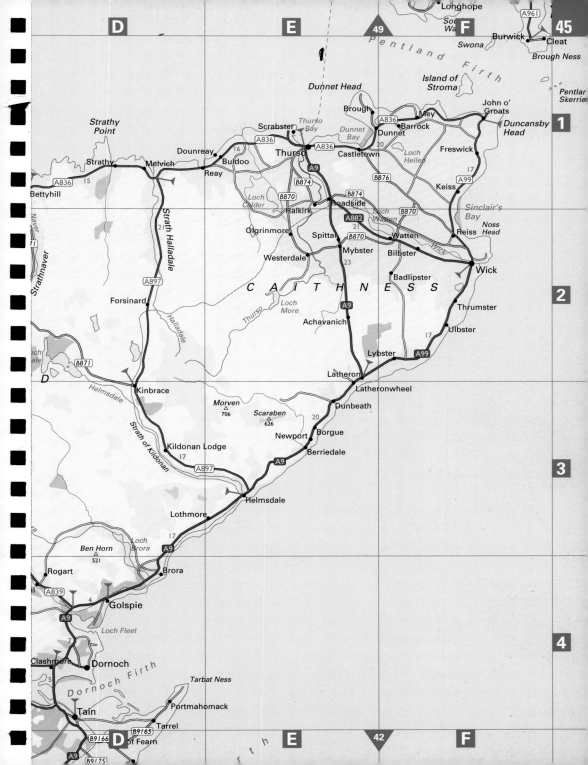

Longhope

A961

Burwick

Cleat

Swona

Brough Ness

Pentland   *Firth*

Island of
Stroma

Pentlar
Skerrie

Dunnet Head

Brough

Mey

John o'
Groats

1

A836

Barrock

Duncansby
Head

Scrabster

*Thurso
Bay*

Dunnet

*Dunnet
Bay*

Castletown

Freswick

Thurso

A836

20

*Loch
Heilen*

Strathy
Point

Strathy

Dounreay

16

A9

B876

Keiss

17

Melvich

Buldoo

Reay

B874

B874

A99

A836

15

*Loch
Calder*

B870

Roadside

B870

*Sinclair's
Bay*

Bettyhill

Halkirk

A882

*Loch
Watten*

Reiss

*Noss
Head*

Naver

21

Olgrinmore

Spittal

B870

Watten

Bilbster

Strathnaver

A897

Strath Halladale

Westerdale

Mybster

Wick

Wick

C A I T H N E S S

23

*Loch
More*

Badlipster

B871

Forsinard

Halladale

Thurso

A9

Achavanich

Thrumster

17

Ulbster

Helmsdale

Lybster

A99

Kinbrace

Latheron

Latheronwheel

Morven
△
706

Scaraben
△
626

20

Dunbeath

Strath of Kildonan

Kildonan Lodge

17

Newport

Borgue

A9

Berriedale

A897

3

Helmsdale

Lothmore

Ben Horn
△
521

*Loch
Brora*

17

A9

Rogart

Brora

A839

4

Golspie

A9

Loch Fleet

4

7

Clashmore

Dornoch

5

Dornoch Firth

Tarbat Ness

Tain

Portmahomack

B9165

Tarrel

B9166

of Fearn

A9

B9175

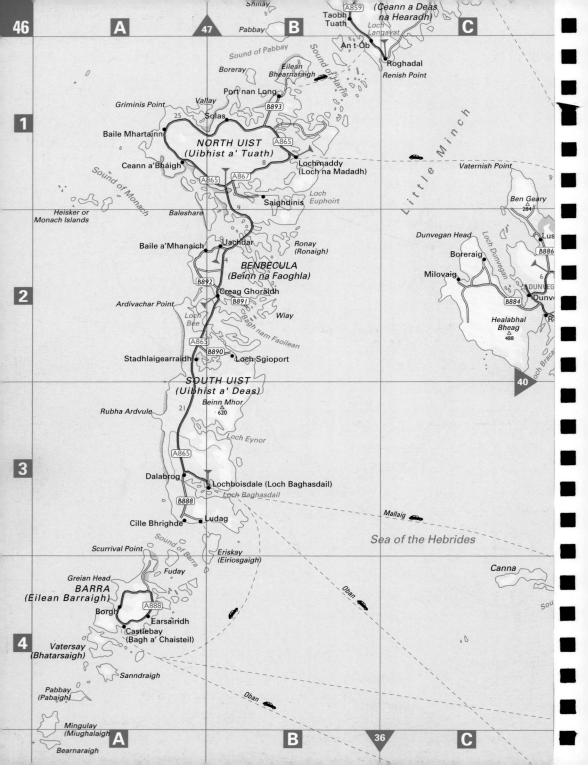

Shillay

Taobh
Tuath

A859

(Ceann a Deas
na Hearadh)

Pabbay

An t-Ob

Loch
Langavat

Sound of Pabbay

Sound of Harris

Roghadal

Renish Point

1

Boreray

Eilean
Bhearnaraigh

Port nan Long

B893

Griminis Point

Vallay

Solas

25

Little Minch

Vaternish Point

Baile Mhartainn

NORTH UIST
(Uibhist a' Tuath)

A865

Ben Geary
284

Ceann a'Bháigh

A865 | A867

8

Lochmaddy
(Loch na Madadh)

Sound of Monach

Baleshare

Saighdinis

Loch
Euphoirt

Dunvegan Head

Loch Dunvegan

Lus

B886

Heisker or
Monach Islands

Boreraig

Milovaig

DUNVEG

Baile a'Mhanaich

Uachdar

Ronay
(Ronaigh)

BENBECULA
(Beinn na Faoghla)

Dunv

B884

2

Ardivachar Point

B892

Creag Ghoraidh

B891

Wiay

Loch
Bee

Bagh nam Faoilean

Healabhal
Bheag
488

R

A865

B890

Stadhlaigearraidh

Loch Sgioport

SOUTH UIST
(Uibhist a' Deas)

40 ▶

Loch Brac

Rubha Ardvule

21

Beinn Mhor
620

Loch Eynor

3

A865

Dalabrog

Lochboisdale (Loch Baghasdail)

B888

Loch Baghasdail

Mallaig

Cille Bhrighde

Ludag

Sea of the Hebrides

Scurrival Point

Sound of Barra

Eriskay
(Eiriosgaigh)

Canna

Greian Head

Fuday

BARRA
(Eilean Barraigh)

Oban

Borgh

A888

Sou

Earsairidh

Vatersay
(Bhatarsaigh)

Castlebay
(Bagh a' Chaisteil)

4

Sanndraigh

Pabbay
(Pabaigh)

Oban

Mingulay
(Miughalaigh)

A | B | 36 ▼ | C

Bearnaraigh

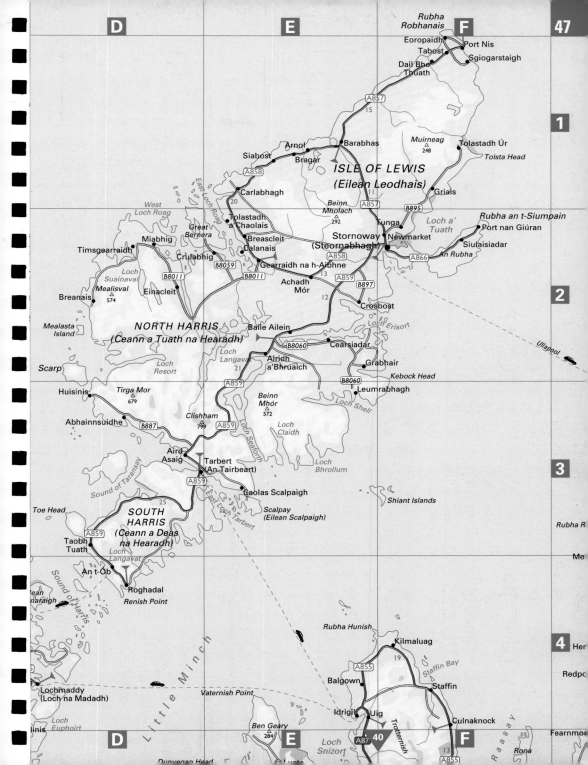

D   E   F

1

2

3

4

Rubha Robhanais
Eoropaidh
Tabost
Dail Bho Thuath
Port Nis
Sgiogarstaigh

A857
15

Arnol
Barabhas
Muirneag △ 248
Tolastadh Úr
Tolsta Head

Siabost
Bragar

ISLE OF LEWIS (Eilean Leodhais)

A858
Carlabhagh
20
West Loch Roag
East Loch Roag

Beinn Mholach △ 292
Tunga
A857
Griais
A895

Tolastadh a'Chaolais
Great Bernera
Breascleit
Calanais
Stornoway (Steornabhagh)
Newmarket
Loch a' Tuath

Rubha an t-Siumpain
Port nan Giúran

Miabhig
Crulabhig
Timsgearraidh
B8059
Gearraidh na h-Aibhne
A858
13
A859
Siulaisiadar
An Rubha
A866

B8011
B8011
Achadh Mór
B897

Breanais
Loch Suainaval
Mealisval △ 574
Einacleit
12
Crosbost

Mealasta Island
NORTH HARRIS (Ceann a Tuath na Hearadh)
Baile Ailein
Loch Erisort

Ullapool

Scarp
Loch Resort
Loch Langavat
B8060
Cearsiadar

Huisinis
Tirga Mor △ 679
Airidh a'Bhruaich
21
A859
Grabhair
Kebock Head
B8060
Leumrabhagh

Abhainnsuidhe
B887
Clishham △ 799
A859
Beinn Mhór △ 572
Loch Shell

Aird Asaig
Tarbert (An-Tairbeart)
A859
Loch Claidh
Loch Seaforth

Sound of Taransay
Loch Bhrollum

Caolas Scalpaigh
Scalpay (Eilean Scalpaigh)
Shiant Islands

Toe Head
25
SOUTH HARRIS (Ceann a Deas na Hearadh)
A859
East Loch Tarbert

Rubha R
Me

Taobh Tuath
A859
Loch Langavat

An t-Òb
Roghadal
Renish Point

Sound of Harris
naraigh

Rubha Hunish
Kilmaluag
19
Her

Little Minch
A855
Staffin Bay

Lochmaddy (Loch na Madadh)
Vaternish Point
Balgown
Staffin
Redpo

inis
Loch Euphoirt
Idrigil
Uig
Trotternish
A87
40
Culnaknock
Raasay
Fearnmor

Ben Geary △ 284
Loch Snizort
13
A855
Rona

D   E   F

Dunvegan Head

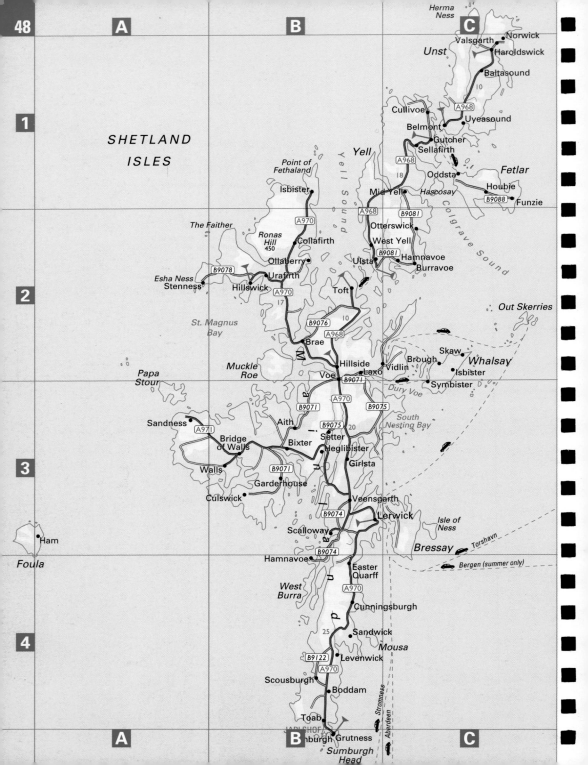

A   B   C

1

2

3

4

A   B   C

SHETLAND ISLES

Herma Ness

Valsgarth   Norwick
Unst   Haroldswick
Baltasound
10

Cullivoe   A968   Uyeasound
Belmont
Gutcher   *Fetlar*
Sellafirth
Yell

Point of Fethaland

Isbister

A968   18   Oddsta   Houbie
Mid Yell   *Hascosay*   B9088   Funzie
The Faither   A970
Ronas Hill 450   Collafirth   A968   Otterswick   B9081
Ollaberry   West Yell
B9078   Urafirth   Ulsta   B9081   Hamnavoe
Esha Ness   Hillswick   Burravoe
Stenness   A970   Toft   *Out Skerries*
17
St. Magnus Bay   10
B9076
Brae   A968   Skaw
Muckle Roe   Hillside   Brough   Isbister   *Whalsay*
Papa Stour   Voe   Laxo   Vidlin   Symbister
B9071   *Dury Voe*
Sandness   A970
A971   B9071   A970   B9075   *South Nesting Bay*
Bridge of Walls   Aith   B9075   20
Bixter   Setter
Walls   B9071   Heglibister
Garderhouse   Girlsta
Culswick   Veensgarth
B9074
Lerwick
Scalloway   *Isle of Ness*
Ham   *Bressay*   Torshavn
Foula   Hamnavoe   B9074
Bergen (summer only)
Easter Quarff
West Burra   A970
Cunningsburgh
25   Sandwick   *Mousa*
B9122   Levenwick
Scousburgh   A970
Boddam
Toab   *Stromness*   *Aberdeen*
JARLSHOF   Grutness
Sumburgh Head

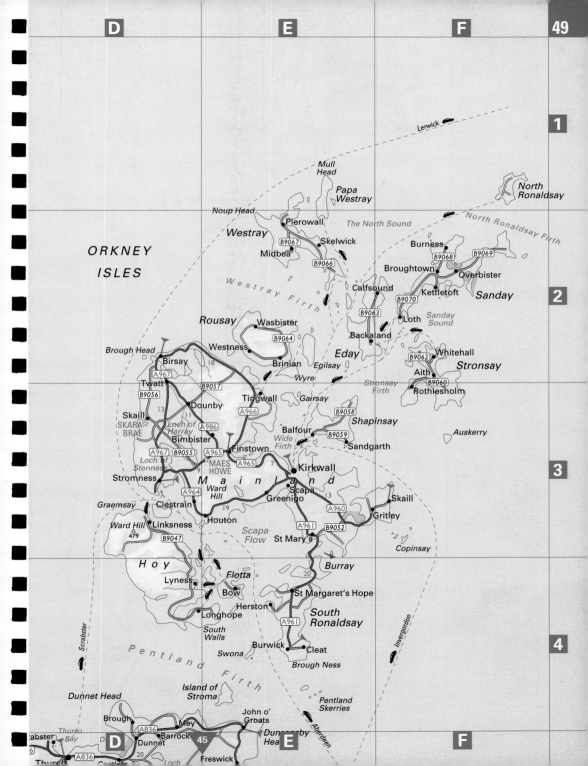

1

Lerwick

Mull
Head

*Papa
Westray*

*North
Ronaldsay*

Noup Head

Pierowall

Westray

Skelwick

The North Sound

B9067

Midbea

B9066

Burness

Broughtown

B9068

B9069

Overbister

North Ronaldsay Firth

ORKNEY
ISLES

Westray Firth

Calfsound

Kettletoft

Sanday

B9070

B9063

Loth

*Sanday
Sound*

2

Rousay

Wasbister

B9064

Backaland

Eday

B9062

Whitehall

Stronsay

Westness

Brinian

Egilsay

Wyre

Aith

B9060

Brough Head

Birsay

18

A967

Twatt

B9057

B9056

Dounby

Tingwall

A966

Gairsay

Rothiesholm

*Stronsay
Firth*

B9058

Shapinsay

Auskerry

Skaill

SKARA
BRAE

13

*Loch of
Harray*

11

A986

Balfour

B9059

Sandgarth

Bimbister

Finstown

A965

*Wide
Firth*

A967

B9055

*Loch of
Stenness*

MAES
HOWE

A965

7

Kirkwall

Stromness

9

Mainland

*Ward
Hill*

Scapa

Greenigo

13

Skaill

A964

19

A960

Gritley

Graemsay

Clestrain

Houton

A961

B9052

Linksness

*Ward Hill
479*

B9047

*Scapa
Flow*

St Mary's

Copinsay

Hoy

Lyness

Flotta

Bow

Burray

20

Brough Ness

Longhope

*South
Walls*

Herston

A961

St Margaret's Hope

*South
Ronaldsay*

Invergordon

3

4

Scrabster

Pentland

Swona

Burwick

Cleat

Firth

Dunnet Head

*Island of
Stroma*

Brough

A836

Mey

Barrock

*John o'
Groats*

Dunnet

45

*Duncansby
Head*

*Pentland
Skerries*

Aberdeen

*Thurso
Bay*

Loch

D

E

F

Freswick

A836

Thurso

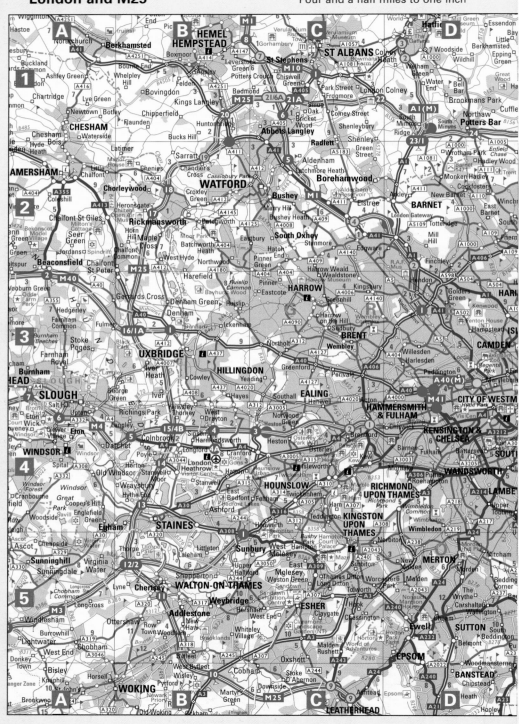

0 1 2 3 4 5 miles
0 1 2 3 4 5 6 7 8 km

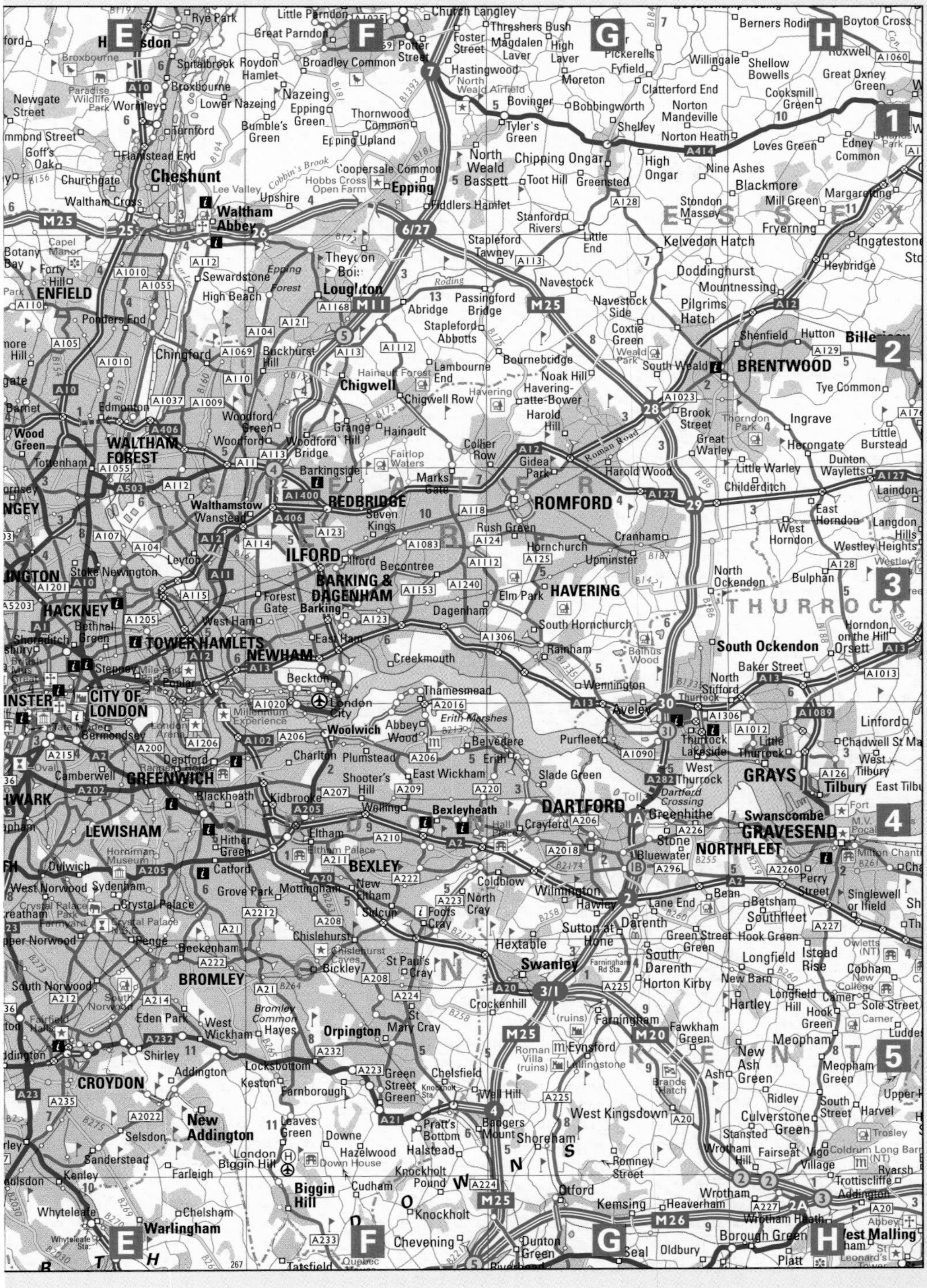

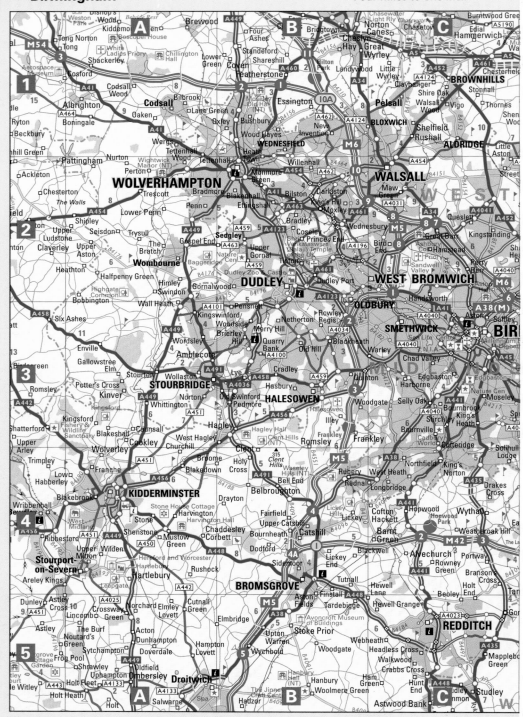

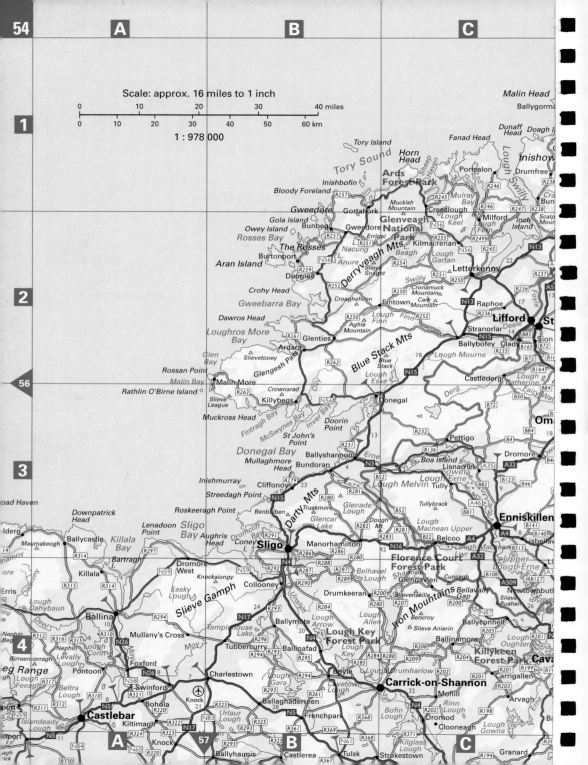

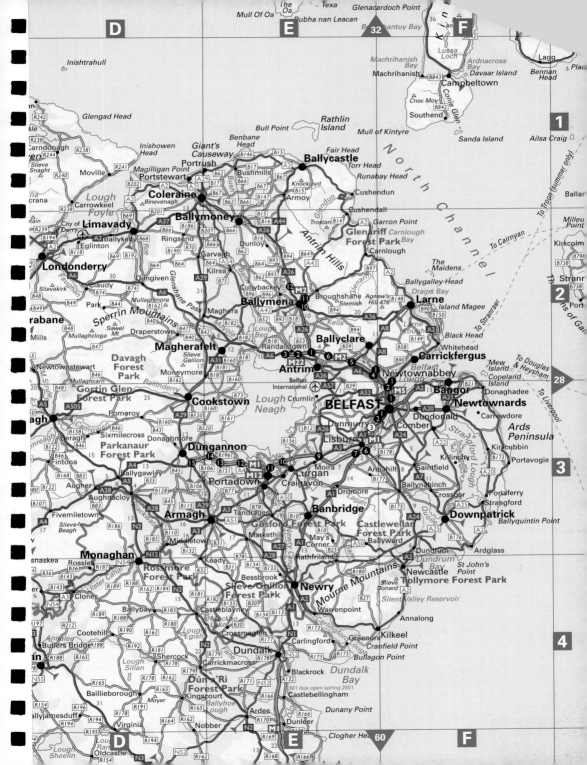

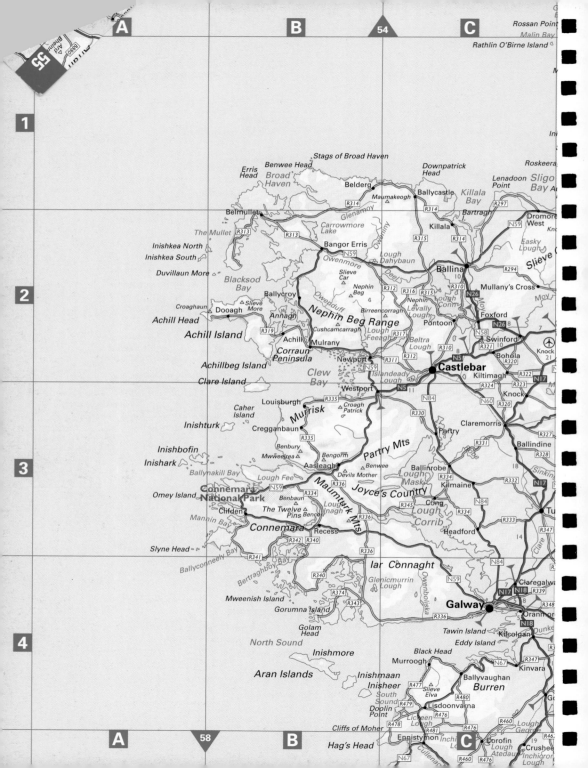

Rossan Point
Malin Bay
Rathlin O'Birne Island

1

Stags of Broad Haven
Erris   Benwee Head
Head   Broad   Belderg   Downpatrick
Haven   Head
Maumakeogh   Ballycastle   Killala
Bay   Lenadoon   Sligo
Point   Bay
R314   R314   Bartragh   N59   Dromore
Belmullet   Glenamoy   Killala   R297   West
Carrowmore   R315   R314   Easky
The Mullet   R313   Lake   Owenmy   Lough
R313   Lough   Slieve
Inishkea North   Bangor Erris   Dahybaun   R294
Inishkea South   N59   Ballina   10
Owenmore   Owenduff   Slieve   Nephin   Mullany's Cross   MoyF
Duvillaun More   Car   Beg   Lough
2   Blacksod   Deels   R312   R316   R315   R310   N26   Foxford
Bay   Ballycroy   Nephin   Nephin   N58   R321   10   Swinford
Lough   Levally   8
Croaghaun   Slieve   Birreencorragh   Lough   Beltra   N58   Knock
More   Annagh   Cushcamcarragh   R317   R310   Bohola   21
Dooagh   Achill   Lough   Lough   R312   R320
Achill Head   Achill   Feeagh   R322   N17
Achill Island   R319   Mulrany   Castlebar   Kiltimagh   R323
Corraun   Newport   R311   R312   Islandeady   R324   Knock
Peninsula   N59   Lough   N5   R320   R327
Achillbeg Island   Westport   N84   N60   Ballindine
Clare Island   Clew   R335   Croagh   R330   Claremorris   R328
Bay   Louisburgh   Patrick   R331   N17
3   Murrisk   Partry   18
Caher   Cregganbaun   R335   Sinking
Island   Benbury   Bengorm   Partry Mts   Lough   R334
Inishturk   Mwweelrea   Benwee   Mask   Kilmaine   R332
Inishbofin   Aasleagh   Devils Mother   Lough   R334
Inishark   Ballynakill Bay   Lough Fee   Joyce's Country   Cong   N84   R333   Tu
Connemara   N59   R334   R345   Lough   R334   R347
Omey Island   National Park   Benbaun   Maumturk   Corrib   Headford   14
Clifden   The Twelve   Mts   R336   Clare
Pins Bencorr   Recess   Iar Connaght   N84
Connemara   R336
Mannin Bay   R342   R340   R336   N59   Claregalwa
Slyne Head   R341   Glenicmurrin   N17   N18   R339
Ballyconneely Bay   Bertraghboy Bay   R340   Lough   Owenboliska   R348
Mweenish Island   R374   Galway   N18   R347
4   Gorumna Island   R343   R336   Oranmor
Golam   Tawin Island   Kilcolgan   Dunke
Head   North Sound   Black Head   Eddy Island   N67   R347
Inishmore   Murrooqh   Ballyvaughan   Kinvara
Aran Islands   Inishmaan   Slieve   Burren
Inisheer   R477   Elva   R480
South   R479   Lisdoonvarna   Licheen
Sound   R476   Lough
Doolin   R478   R481   R476   R460   Lough
Point   Lickeen   N67
Cliffs of Moher   Lough   Ennistymon   Inch   Corofin   R46
Hag's Head   N67   R460   R476   Crushee
Cullenagh   Inchicro
Lough   Lough

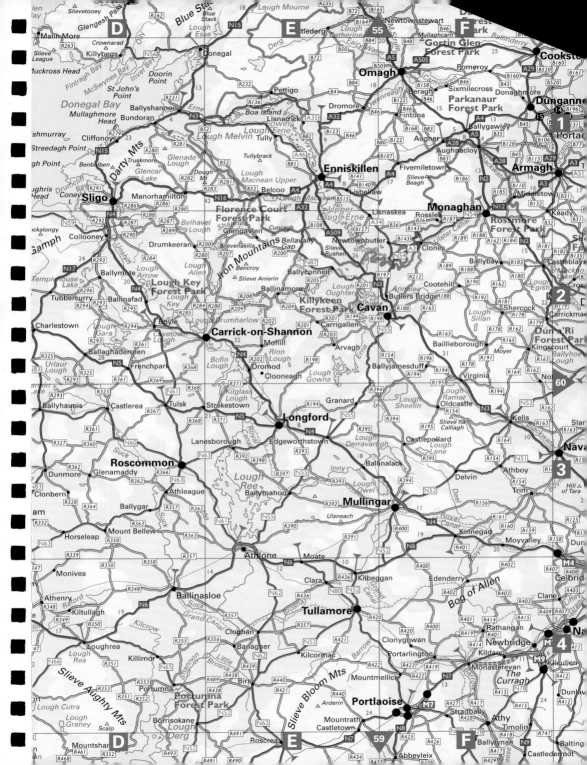

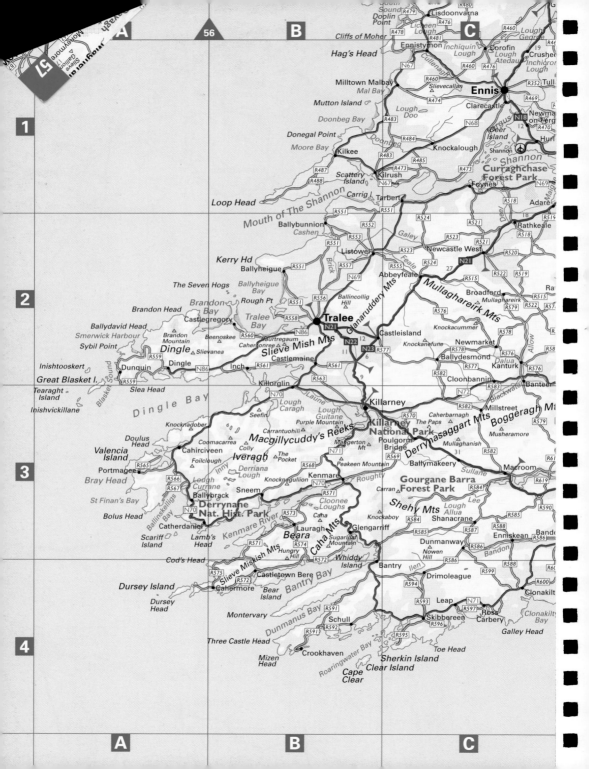

Abbreviations

Aber.	Aberdeenshire	*Glos.*	Gloucestershire	*Nhumb.*	Northumberland	*Stir.*	Stirling
Arg. & B.	Argyll & Bute	*Gt.Lon.*	Greater London	*Norf.*	Norfolk	*Suff.*	Suffolk
B'burn.	Blackburn with	*Gt.Man.*	Greater Manchester	*Northants.*	Northamptonshire	*Surr.*	Surrey
	Darwen	*Hants.*	Hampshire	*Notts.*	Nottinghamshire	*Swin.*	Swindon
Beds.	Bedfordshire	*Here.*	Herefordshire	*Ork.*	Orkney	*T. & W.*	Tyne & Wear
Brack.F.	Bracknell Forest	*Herts.*	Hertfordshire	*Oxon.*	Oxfordshire	*Tel. & W.*	Telford and Wrekin
Bucks.	Buckinghamshire	*High.*	Highland	*P. & K.*	Perth & Kinross	*Thur.*	Thurrock
Caerp.	Caerphilly	*I.o.M.*	Isle of Man	*Pembs.*	Pembrokeshire	*V. of Glam.*	Vale of Glamorgan
Cambs.	Cambridgeshire	*I.o.W.*	Isle of Wight	*Peter.*	Peterborough	*W'ham.*	Wokingham
Ches.	Cheshire	*Lancs.*	Lancashire	*R.C.T.*	Rhondda Cynon Taff	*W. & M.*	Windsor &
Cornw.	Cornwall	*Leics.*	Leicestershire	*Renf.*	Renfrewshire		Maidenhead
Cumb.	Cumbria	*Lincs.*	Lincolnshire	*S.Ayr.*	South Ayrshire	*W.Isles*	Western Isles
D. & G.	Dumfries & Galloway	*M.K.*	Milton Keynes	*S.Glos.*	South Gloucestershire	*W.Loth.*	West Lothian
Derbys.	Derbyshire	*Med.*	Medway	*S.Lan.*	South Lanarkshire	*W.Mid.*	West Midlands
Dur.	Durham	*Mersey.*	Merseyside	*S.Yorks.*	South Yorkshire	*W.Suss.*	West Sussex
E.Ayr.	East Ayrshire	*Midloth.*	Midlothian	*Sc.Bord.*	Scottish Borders	*W.Yorks.*	West Yorkshire
E.Loth.	East Lothian	*Mon.*	Monmouthshire	*Shet.*	Shetland	*Warks.*	Warwickshire
E.Riding	East Riding of	*N.Lan.*	North Lanarkshire	*Shrop.*	Shropshire	*Warr.*	Warrington
	Yorkshire	*N.Lincs.*	North Lincolnshire	*Slo.*	Slough	*Wilts.*	Wiltshire
E.Suss.	East Sussex	*N.P.T.*	Neath & Port Talbot	*Som.*	Somerset	*Worcs.*	Worcestershire
Flints.	Flintshire	*N.Yorks.*	North Yorkshire	*Staffs.*	Staffordshire	*Wrex.*	Wrexham

Bold entries refer to Urban Area Maps pages 50-53.

Abbey Wood 51 F4
Abbeytown 29 E2
Abbots Bromley 20 C3
Abbots Langley 50 C1
Abbotsbury 8 A4
Aberaeron 12 B3
Aberaman 7 D1
Aberavon 6 C1
Abercanaid 7 E1
Aberchirder 43 D2
Abercynon 7 E1
Aberdare 7 D1
Aberdaron 18 A3
Aberdeen 43 F4
Aberdeen Airport 43 E4
Aberdour 34 B1
Aberdyfi 12 C1
Aberfeldy 38 B2
Aberffraw 18 A2
Aberfoyle 38 A4
Abergavenny 7 E1
Abergele 19 D1
Abergynolwyn 12 C1
Aberkenfig 7 D2
Aberlady 34 C1
Aberlemno 39 E2
Aberlour 42 C3
Abernethy 38 C4
Aberporth 12 A3
Abersoch 18 A3
Abersychan 7 E1
Abertillery 7 E1
Aberuthven 38 C4
Aberystwyth 12 C2
Abhainnsuidhe 47 D3
Abingdon 15 D4
Abington 34 A3
Aboyne 43 D4
Abram 25 D4
Abridge 51 F2
Accrington 25 E3
Achadh Mór 47 E2
Achahoish 32 C1
Acharacle 36 C2
Achavanich 45 E2
Achfary 44 B2
Achiltibuie 44 A3
Achintee 41 D3

Achnacroish 37 D3
Achnasheen 41 E2
Achosnich 36 C2
Achriesgill 44 B2
Ackworth Moor Top 26 A3
Acle 23 F3
Acock's Green 53 D3
Acomb 30 B1
Acton Gt.Lon. 50 C4
Acton Worcs. 52 A5
Adderbury 15 D2
Addingham 25 F2
Addington 51 E5
Addlestone 10 A2
Addlestone 50 B5
Adlington 25 D3
Adwick le Street 26 B3
Ainsdale 24 C3
Aintree 24 C4
Aird Asaig 47 D3
Aird of Sleat 40 B4
Airdrie 34 A2
Airidh a'Bhruaich 47 E2
Airth 34 A1
Airton 25 E1
Aith Ork. 49 F2
Aith Shet. 48 B3
Akeld 35 E3
Albrighton 20 B3
Albrighton 52 A1
Alcester 14 C1
Aldbourne 14 C4
Aldbrough 27 D2
Aldeburgh 17 F2
Aldenham 16 A4
Aldenham 50 C2
Alderbury 8 C2
Alderholt 8 C3
Alderley Edge 20 B1
Alderman's Green 53 F3
Aldershot 9 F1
Aldingham 24 C1
Aldington 11 E3
Aldridge 20 B4
Aldridge 52 C1
Alexandria 33 E1
Alford *Aber.* 43 D4

Alford *Lincs.* 22 B1
Alfreton 21 D1
Allanton *N.Lan.* 34 A2
Allendale Town 30 B2
Allenheads 30 B2
Allesley 53 E3
Allhallows 11 D1
Allnabad 44 C2
Alloa 34 A1
Allonby 29 E2
Alloway 33 E3
Almondsbury 14 A4
Alness 42 A2
Alnmouth 35 F4
Alnwick 35 F4
Alresford 17 D3
Alrewas 20 C3
Alsager 20 B1
Alston 30 A2
Altnafeadh 37 F2
Altnaharra 44 C2
Alton *Hants.* 9 F2
Alton *Staffs.* 20 C2
Altrincham 25 E4
Alva 38 B4
Alveley 20 A4
Alves 42 B2
Alveston 14 A4
Alvie 42 A4
Alyth 39 D2
Ambergate 21 D2
Amble 35 F4
Amblecote 20 B4
Amblecote 52 A3
Ambleside 29 F4
Ambrosden 15 E3
Amersham 15 F3
Amersham 50 A2
Amesbury 8 C2
Amington 53 E1
Amlwch 18 B1
Ammanford 6 C1
Ampthill 15 F2
Amulree 38 B3
An t-Ob 47 D4

An Tairbeart 47 E3
Ancaster 21 F2
Ancroft 35 E2
Ancrum 35 D3
Andover 9 D1
Andreas 24 B2
Angle 12 A2
Angmering 10 A4
Anlaby 27 D3
Annan 29 E1
Annbank 33 E3
Annfield Plain 30 C2
Ansley 53 E2
Anstey 21 D3
Anstruther 39 E4
Ansty 53 F3
Aoradh 32 A2
Appleby Magna 20 C3
Appleby Parva 53 F1
Appleby-in-Westmorland 30 A3
Applecross 40 C3
Appledore *Devon* 6 B4
Appledore *Kent* 11 E3
Appleton Thorn 19 F1
Appley Bridge 25 D3
Arbirlot 39 E3
Arbroath 39 E3
Ardchiavaig 36 B4
Arden 33 E1
Ardentinny 33 E1
Ardeonaig 38 A3
Ardersier 42 A2
Ardfern 37 D4
Ardgay 44 C4
Ardleigh 17 D3
Ardlui 37 F4
Ardlussa 32 B1
Ardmair 41 D1
Ardminish 32 B2
Ardmolich 37 D1
Ardrishaig 32 C1
Ardrossan 33 E3
Ardtalnaig 38 A3
Ardtoe 36 C2
Ardvasar 40 C4
Arinagour 36 B2

Arisaig 36 C1
Arkley 50 D2
Armadale 34 A1
Armitage 20 C3
Armthorpe 26 B4
Arncliffe 25 E1
Arnisdale 40 C4
Arnol 47 E1
Arnold 21 E2
Arnprior 38 A4
Arrochar 37 F4
Arundel 10 A4
Ascot 9 F1
Ascot 50 A5
Asfordby 21 E3
Ash *Kent* 51 H5
Ash *Kent* 11 F2
Ash *Surr.* 9 F1
Ashbourne 20 C2
Ashburton 5 D2
Ashbury 14 C4
Ashby de la Zouch 21 D3
Ashchurch 14 B2
Ashcott 7 F3
Ashford *Kent* 11 E2
Ashford *Surr.* 10 A1
Ashford *Surr.* 50 B4
Ashington 31 D1
Ashkirk 34 C3
Ashley *Cambs.* 16 C1
Ashley Green 50 A1
Ashow 53 F4
Ashton 19 F2
Ashton-in-Makerfield 25 D4
Ashton-under-Lyne 25 E4
Ashurst *E.Suss.* 10 C3
Ashurst *Hants.* 9 D3
Ashwick 8 A1
Askern 26 B3
Aspatria 29 E2
Astley *Warks.* 53 F3
Aston *W.Mid.* 52 C3
Aston Clinton 15 F3
Aston Fields 52 B4

Aston on Trent 21 D2
Astwood Bank 14 B1
Astwood Bank 52 C5
Atherington 6 C4
Atherstone 20 C4
Atherstone 53 F2
Atherton 25 D4
Attadale 41 D3
Attleborough *Norf.* 23 D4
Attleborough *Warks.* 53 F2
Attlebridge 23 E3
Auchallater 38 C1
Auchenblae 39 E1
Auchenbreck 33 D1
Auchencairn 29 D2
Auchencrow 35 E2
Auchindrain 37 E4
Auchinleck 33 F3
Auchmull 39 E1
Auchnagatt 43 F3
Aucholzie 39 D1
Auchterarder 38 B4
Auchtermuchty 39 D4
Auchtertool 34 B1
Audlem 20 A2
Audley 20 A2
Aughton *Lancs.* 24 C4
Aughton *S.Yorks.* 26 A4
Auldearn 42 B2
Aultbea 41 D1
Aultguish Inn 41 E2
Austrey 53 E1
Aveley 10 C1
Aveley 51 G3
Aviemore 42 B4
Avoch 42 A2
Avonbridge 34 A1
Avonmouth 7 F2
Awre 14 A3
Awsworth 21 D2
Axminster 5 F1
Aycliffe 31 D3
Aylesbury 15 E3
Aylesford 11 D2
Aylesham 11 F2
Aylsham 23 E3
Ayr 33 E3
Aysgarth 30 C4

B

Babworth 26 B4
Backaland 49 E2
Backwell 7 F2
Bacup 25 E3
Badcaul 41 D1
Baddesley Ensor 53 E2
Badenscoth 43 E3
Badgers Mount 51 F5
Badlipster 45 F2
Badsey 14 B2
Bagh a' Chaisteil (Castlebay) 46 A4
Bagillt 19 E1
Baginton 53 F4
Baglan 6 C1
Bagshot 9 F1
Baildon 25 F2
Baile Ailein 47 E2
Baile a'Mhanaich 46 A2
Baile Mhartainn 46 A1
Baile Mòr 36 B3
Bainbridge 30 B4
Bainton 26 C2
Baker Street 51 H3

Bala 19 D3
Balbeggie 38 C3
Balblair 42 A2
Balcombe 10 B3
Balderton 21 E2
Baldslow 11 D4
Balemartine 36 A3
Balephuil 36 A3
Balfour 49 E3
Balfron 33 F1
Balgown 40 B2
Balgray 39 D3
Balintore 42 A2
Ballabeg 24 A3
Ballachulish 37 E2
Ballantrae 28 A1
Ballasalla 24 A3
Ballater 39 D1
Ballaugh 24 A2
Ballingry 38 C4
Ballinluig 38 C2
Ballintuim 38 C2
Balloch 33 E1
Ballochroy 32 C2
Ballygrant 32 A2
Balmacara 40 C3
Balmaha 33 E1
Balmedie 43 F4
Balnacra 41 D3
Balnahard 36 C3
Balnapaling 42 A2
Balquhidder 38 A3
Balsall 53 E4
Balsall Common 53 E4
Baltasound 48 C1
Balvicar 37 D4
Bamburgh 35 F3
Bampton *Devon* 7 D4
Bampton *Oxon.* 14 C3
Banbury 15 D2
Banchory 39 E1
Banff 43 E2
Bangor 18 B1
Banham 23 D4
Bankfoot 38 C3
Bannockburn 34 A1
Banstead 10 B2
Banwell 7 F3
Bar Hill 16 B1
Barabhas 47 E1
Barassie 33 E3
Barbaraville 42 A2
Barbon 25 D1
Barby 15 D1
Bardney 22 A1
Bardsea 24 C1
Bargoed 7 E1
Bargrennan 28 B1
Barham 11 F2
Barking *Gt.Lon.* 51 F3
Barking & Dagenham 51 F3
Barkingside 51 F3
Barkston 21 F2
Barlaston 20 B2
Barlborough 21 D1
Barley 16 B2
Barmouth 12 C1
Barnacle 53 F3
Barnard Castle 30 C3
Barnes 50 D4
Barnet 50 D2
Barningham 17 D1
Barnoldswick 25 E2
Barnsley 26 A4

Barnstaple 6 C4
Barnt Green 52 C4
Barnton 20 A1
Barr 33 E4
Barrapol 36 A3
Barrhead 33 F2
Barrhill 28 B1
Barrock 45 F1
Barrow upon Humber 27 D3
Barrow upon Soar 21 E3
Barrow-in-Furness 24 B1
Barrowford 25 E2
Barry 7 E2
Barston 53 E4
Barton (Preston) *Lancs.* 25 D2
Barton in the Beans 53 F1
Barton-le-Clay 16 A3
Barton-under-Needwood 20 C3
Barton-upon-Humber 27 D3
Baschurch 19 F3
Basildon 11 D1
Basingstoke 9 E1
Baslow 20 C1
Bassingham 21 F1
Batchworth 50 B2
Batchworth Heath 50 B2
Bath 8 B1
Batheaston 8 B1
Bathford 8 B1
Bathgate 34 A1
Batley 25 F3
Battersea 50 D4
Battle 11 D4
Bawdeswell 23 D3
Bawdsey 17 E2
Bawtry 26 B4
Baxterley 53 E2
Baycliff 24 C1
Bayford *Herts.* 51 E1
Bayston Hill 13 F1
Beaconsfield 10 A1
Beaconsfield 50 A2
Beadnell 35 F3
Beaminster 5 F1
Bean 51 G4
Bearsden 33 F1
Bearsted 11 D2
Beattock 34 B4
Beauchamp Roding 51 G1
Beaudesert 53 D5
Beauly 41 F3
Beaumaris 18 B1
Beausale 53 E4
Bebington 19 E1
Beccles 23 F4
Beckenham 51 E5
Beckingham 26 C4
Beckton 51 F3
Becontree 51 F3
Bedale 31 D4
Beddau 7 D2
Beddgelert 18 B2
Beddingham 10 C4
Beddington 51 E5
Beddington Corner 50 D5
Bedford 15 F2
Bedlington 30 C1
Bedmond 50 C1

Bedwas 7 E2
Bedworth 21 D4
Bedworth 53 F3
Beeford 27 D2
Beer 5 E1
Beeston *Notts.* 21 D2
Beighton *S.Yorks.* 26 A4
Beith 33 E2
Belbroughton 20 B4
Belbroughton 52 B4
Belford 35 F3
Bell Bar 50 D1
Bell End 52 B4
Bellingdon 50 A1
Bellingham 30 B1
Bellshill *N.Lan.* 33 F2
Belmont *Gt.Lon.* 50 D5
Belmont *Shet.* 48 C1
Belper 21 D2
Belsay 30 C1
Belvedere 51 F4
Bembridge 9 E4
Bempton 27 D1
Benenden 11 D3
Benllech 18 B1
Benson 15 E4
Bentley *S.Yorks.* 26 B4
Bentley *Warks.* 53 E2
Bentley Heath 53 D4
Beoley 52 C5
Bere Alston 4 B2
Bere Ferrers 4 B2
Bere Regis 8 B3
Berinsfield 15 D4
Berkeley 14 A3
Berkhamsted 15 F3
Berkhamsted 50 A1
Berkswell 20 C4
Berkswell 53 E4
Bermondsey 51 E4
Berners Roding 51 H1
Bernisdale 40 B2
Berriedale 45 E3
Berrow 7 E3
Bersham 19 E2
Berwick-upon-Tweed 35 E2
Bessacarr 26 B4
Bethersden 11 E3
Bethesda 18 B2
Bethnal Green 51 E3
Betsham 51 H4
Bettyhill 44 C1
Betws-y-coed 18 C2
Beverley 27 D2
Bewdley 20 A4
Bexhill 11 D4
Bexley 51 F4
Bexleyheath 51 F4
Bibury 14 C3
Bicester 15 E3
Bickenhill 53 D3
Bickleigh (Plymouth) *Devon* 4 C2
Bickleigh (Tiverton) *Devon* 5 D1
Bickley 51 F5
Bicknacre 16 C4
Biddenden 11 D3
Biddulph 20 B1
Bideford 6 B4
Bidford-on-Avon 14 C1
Bigbury-on-Sea 4 C3
Biggar 34 A3
Biggin Hill 10 C2
Biggleswade 16 A2

Bilbrook *Staffs.* 52 A1
Bilbster 45 F2
Billericay 16 C4
Billinge 25 D4
Billingham 31 D3
Billinghay 22 A2
Billingshurst 10 A3
Billockby 23 F3
Billy Row 30 C2
Bilston *Midloth.* 34 B2
Bilston *W.Mid.* 52 B2
Bilstone 53 F1
Bilton 27 D3
Bimbister 49 E3
Binbrook 27 D4
Binfield 9 F1
Bingham 21 E2
Bingley 25 F2
Binley *W.Mid.* 53 F4
Birchgrove *N.P.T.* 6 C1
Birchington 11 F1
Bircotes 26 B4
Bird End 52 C2
Birkenhead 19 E1
Birmingham 20 C4
Birmingham 52 C3
Birmingham International Airport 20 C4
Birmingham International Airport 53 D3
Birsay 49 D2
Birstall 21 E3
Birtley *T. & W.* 31 D2
Bishop Auckland 30 C3
Bishopbriggs 33 F1
Bishop's Castle 13 F2
Bishop's Cleeve 14 B2
Bishop's Hull 7 E4
Bishop's Itchington 15 D1
Bishop's Lydeard 7 E4
Bishop's Stortford 16 B3
Bishop's Tawton 6 C4
Bishop's Waltham 9 E3
Bishop's Wood 52 A1
Bishopston 6 C1
Bishopton *Renf.* 33 F1
Bisley 14 B3
Bitton 8 A1
Bixter 48 B3
Blaby 21 D4
Black Bourton 14 C3
Black Notley 16 C3
Blackburn *Aber.* 43 E4
Blackburn *B'burn.* 25 D3
Blackburn *W.Loth.* 34 A2
Blackford 38 B4
Blackhall Colliery 31 D2
Blackheath *W.Mid.* 52 B3
Blacklunans 38 C2
Blackmoor Gate 6 C3
Blackmore 51 H1
Blackpool 24 C2
Blackpool Airport 24 C3
Blackridge 34 A1
Blackwaterfoot 32 C3
Blackwell *Worcs.* 52 B4
Blackwood 7 E1
Blaenau Ffestiniog 18 C2
Blaenavon 7 E1
Blaengarw 7 D1
Blaengwrach 7 D1
Blagdon 7 F3

Blaich 37 E1
Blaina 7 E1
Blair Atholl 38 B2
Blairgowrie 38 C3
Blakebrook 52 A4
Blakedown 52 A4
Blakeney *Glos.* 14 A3
Blakeney *Norf.* 23 D2
Blakenhall *W.Mid.* 52 B2
Blakeshall 52 A3
Blandford Forum 8 B3
Blaydon 30 C1
Blean 11 E2
Bletchley 15 F2
Blewbury 15 D4
Blisworth 15 E1
Blockley 14 C2
Blossomfield 53 D4
Bloxham 15 D2
Bloxwich 52 B1
Blubberhouses 25 F2
Blyth *Nhumb.* 31 D1
Blyth *Notts.* 26 B4
Blyth Bridge 34 B2
Blyton 26 C4
Boat of Garten 42 B4
Boath 41 F2
Bobbington 52 A2
Bobbingworth 51 G1
Boddam *Aber.* 43 F3
Boddam *Shet.* 48 B4
Bodelwyddan 19 D1
Bodenham 13 F3
Bodicote 15 D2
Bodmin 4 A2
Bogniebrae 43 D3
Bognor Regis 9 F3
Boldon 31 D2
Boldre 9 D3
Bollington (Macclesfield)
   Ches. 20 B1
Bolnhurst 16 A1
Bolsover 21 D1
Boltby 31 D4
Bolton *E.Loth.* 34 C1
Bolton *Gt.Man.* 25 D3
Bolton-le-Sands 24 C1
Bolventor 4 A2
Bonar Bridge 44 C4
Bonawe 37 E3
Bonawe Quarries 37 E3
Bonchester Bridge 35 D4
Bonehill 53 D1
Bo'ness 34 A1
Boningale 52 A1
Bonjedward 35 D3
Bonnybridge 34 A1
Bonnyrigg 34 C2
Bonvilston 7 E2
Bootle *Cumb.* 29 E4
Bootle *Mersey.* 19 E1
Boreham 16 C3
Borehamwood 16 A4
Borehamwood 50 C2
Boreland 34 B4
Boreraig 40 A2
Borgh 46 A4
Borgue *D. & G.* 28 C2
Borgue *High.* 45 E3
Borough Green 10 C2
Boroughbridge 26 A1
Borrowash 21 D2
Borrowdale 29 F3
Borth 12 C2
Borve 40 B3
Bosbury 14 A2
Boscastle 4 A1

Bosham 9 F3
Boston 22 A2
Boston Spa 26 A2
Botany Bay 50 D2
Botesdale 17 D1
Bothel 29 E2
Bothenhampton 5 F1
Botley *Bucks.* 50 A1
Bottesford *Leics.* 21 E2
Bottesford *N.Lincs.*
   26 C3
Boughton 21 E1
Bournbrook 52 C3
Bourne 22 A3
Bourne End *Bucks.*
   15 F4
**Bourne End *Herts.*
   50 B1**
Bournebridge 51 G2
Bournemouth 8 C3
Bournemouth
   International Airport
   8 C3
Bournheath 52 B4
Bournmoor 31 D2
Bournville 52 C3
Bourton 8 B2
Bourton-on-the-Water
   14 C3
Boveney 50 A4
Bovey Tracey 5 D2
Bovingdon 50 B1
Bovinger 51 G1
Bow 49 E4
Bowburn 31 D2
Bowes 30 B3
Bowmore 32 A2
Bowness-on-Solway
   29 E1
Bowness-on-Windermere
   29 F4
Box 8 B1
Boxmoor 50 B1
Boyton Cross 51 H1
Bozeat 15 F1
Braaid 24 A3
Bracadale 40 A3
Bracebridge Heath 21 F1
Brackley 15 E2
Bracknell 9 F1
Braco 38 B4
Bracora 37 D1
Bradford *W.Yorks.* 25 F2
Bradford-on-Avon 8 B1
Brading 9 E4
Bradley *W.Mid.* 52 B2
Bradmore *W.Mid.* 52 A2
Bradninch 5 E1
Bradpole 5 F1
Bradshaw 25 D3
Bradwell *Derbys.* 25 F4
Bradwell *Norf.* 23 F4
Bradwell Waterside
   17 D3
Brae 48 B2
Braeantra 41 F1
Braemar 38 C1
Bragar 47 E1
Brailsford 20 C2
Braintree 16 C3
Braithwaite 29 E3
Braithwell 26 B4
Bramford 17 E2
Bramhall 25 E4
Bramley *S.Yorks.* 26 A4
Brampton *Cambs.* 16 A1
Brampton *Cumb.* 30 A2

Brampton *Suff.* 17 F1
Brancaster 22 C2
Brandesburton 27 D2
Brandon *Dur.* 30 C2
Brandon *Suff.* 22 C4
Branson's Cross 52 C4
Branston 21 F1
Brantham 17 E2
Bratton 8 B1
Braunston 15 D1
Braunstone 21 D3
Braunton 6 B4
Bray 10 A1
Brayton 26 B3
Breage 3 E3
Breakish 40 C4
Bream 14 A3
Breanais 47 D2
Breascleit 47 E2
Breaston 21 D2
Brechfa 12 B4
Brechin 39 E2
Brecon 13 E2
Bredbury 25 E4
Bredon 14 B2
Brent 50 C3
Brentford 50 C4
Brentwood 51 G2
Bretton 19 E2
Brewood 20 B3
Brewood 52 A1
Bricket Wood 50 C1
Bridge 11 E2
Bridge of Allan 38 B4
Bridge of Balgie 38 A2
Bridge of Cally 38 C2
Bridge of Craigisla 39 D2
Bridge of Don 43 F4
Bridge of Dun 39 E2
Bridge of Dye 39 E1
Bridge of Earn 38 C4
Bridge of Orchy 37 F3
Bridge of Walls 48 B3
Bridge of Weir 33 F2
Bridgend *Angus* 39 E2
Bridgend *Bridgend* 7 D2
Bridgend *Moray* 42 C3
Bridgend (Islay)
   Arg. & B. 32 A2
Bridgend (Lochgilphead)
   Arg. & B. 32 C1
Bridgnorth 20 A4
Bridgtown 52 B1
Bridgwater 7 E4
Bridlington 27 D1
Bridport 5 F1
Brierfield 25 E2
Brierley Hill 52 B3
Brig o'Turk 38 A4
Brigg 26 C3
Brigham 29 E3
Brighouse 25 F3
Brightstone 9 D4
Brightlingsea 17 D3
Brighton 10 B4
Brigstock 21 F4
Brimington 21 D1
Brinian 49 E2
Brinsley 21 D2
Brinsworth 26 A4
Bristol 14 A4
Bristol International
   Airport 7 F2
Briston 23 D3
Briton Ferry 6 C1
Brixham 5 D3

Brixworth 15 E1
Broad Haven 12 A2
Broad Oak 11 D3
Broadclyst 5 D1
Broadford 40 C4
Broadheath 14 A1
**Broadley Common
   51 F1**
Broadmayne 8 B4
Broadstairs 11 F2
Broadway 14 C2
Broadwey 8 A4
Broadwindsor 5 F1
Brochel 40 B3
Brockenhurst 9 D3
Brockworth 14 B3
Brodick 33 D3
Brodsworth 26 B4
Bromham *Beds.* 15 F1
Bromham *Wilts.* 8 C1
Bromley 51 F5
Brompton 31 D4
Brompton on Swale
   30 C4
Bromsgrove 14 B1
Bromsgrove 52 B4
Bromyard 14 A1
Bronaber 18 C3
**Brook Street *Essex*
   51 G2**
Brooke 23 E4
Brookmans Park 16 A4
Brookmans Park 50 D1
Broome *Worcs.* 52 B4
Broomfield 16 C3
Brora 45 D4
Broseley 20 A4
Brotton 31 E3
Brough *Cumb.* 30 B3
Brough *E.Riding* 26 C3
Brough *High.* 45 E1
Brough *Shet.* 48 C2
Broughton *Flints.* 19 E2
Broughton *N.Lincs.*
   26 C3
Broughton *Northants.*
   21 F4
Broughton *Sc.Bord.*
   34 B3
Broughton Astley 21 D4
Broughton in Furness
   29 E4
Broughtown 49 F2
Broughty Ferry 39 E3
Brownhills *W.Mid.* 20 B3
Brownhills *W.Mid.* 52 C1
Brownshill Green 53 F3
Broxbourne 51 E1
Broxburn 34 B1
Brundall 23 E3
Brundish 17 E1
Bruton 8 A2
Brynamman 6 C1
Brynford 19 E1
Brynmawr 7 E1
Bubbenhall 53 F4
Bubwith 26 B2
Buchlyvie 33 F1
Buckden *Cambs.* 16 A1
Buckden *N.Yorks.* 25 E1
Buckfastleigh 4 C2
Buckhaven 39 D4
Buckhurst Hill 51 F2
Buckie 43 D2
Buckingham 15 E2
**Buckland Common
   50 A1**
Bucklebury 9 E1

Buckley 19 E2
Bucks Hill 50 B1
Bucksburn 43 E4
Budbrooke 53 E5
Bude 4 A1
Budleigh Salterton 5 E2
Bugbrooke 15 E1
Builth Wells 13 D3
Buldoo 45 E1
Bulford 8 C2
Bulkington *Warks.* 21 D4
**Bulkington *Warks.*
   53 F3**
Bulmer Tye 17 D2
Bulphan 51 H3
Bumble's Green 51 F1
Bunessan 36 B3
Bungay 23 E4
Buntingford 16 B3
Burbage 9 D1
Bures 17 D2
Burford 14 C3
Burgess Hill 10 B3
Burgh by Sands 29 F2
Burgh le Marsh 22 B1
Burghead 42 B2
Burghfield Common
   9 E1
Burghill 13 F3
Burley 9 D3
Burley in Wharfdale
   25 F2
Burness 49 F2
Burnham *Bucks.* 10 A1
Burnham *Bucks.* 50 A3
Burnham Market 22 C2
Burnham-on-Crouch
   17 D4
Burnham-on-Sea 7 E3
Burnhouse 33 E2
Burniston 31 F4
Burnley 25 E2
Burnmouth 35 E2
Burnopfield 30 C2
Burntisland 34 B1
Burntwood Green 20 C3
Burntwood Green 52 C1
Burravoe 48 C2
Burrelton 38 C3
Burrowhill 50 A5
Burry Port 6 B1
Burscough 24 C3
Burscough Bridge 24 C3
Bursledon 9 E3
Burton Bradstock 5 F1
**Burton Green *Warks.*
   53 E4**
Burton Joyce 21 E2
Burton Latimer 15 F1
Burton Leonard 26 A1
Burton upon Stather
   26 C3
Burton upon Trent 20 C3
Burton-in-Kendal 25 D1
Burwardsley 19 F2
Burwarton 20 A4
Burwash 11 D3
Burwell 16 B1
Burwick 49 E4
Bury 25 E3
Bury St. Edmunds 17 D1
Bushbury 52 B1
Bushey 16 A4
Bushey 50 C2
Bushey Heath 50 C2
Buttermere 29 E3
Butterwick 26 C1

Buxted 10 C3
Buxton 20 B1
Byfield 15 D1
Byfleet 10 A2
Byfleet 50 B5
Bylchau 19 D2

C

Caerau *Cardiff* 7 E2
Caergwrle 19 E2
Caerhun 18 C1
Caerleon 7 F1
Caernarfon 18 B2
Caerphilly 7 E2
Caerwent 7 F1
Cairnbaan 32 C1
Cairndow 37 E4
Cairneyhill 34 A1
Cairnryan 28 A1
Caister-on-Sea 23 F3
Caistor 27 D4
Calanais 47 E2
Caldbeck 29 F2
Caldecote *Warks.* 53 F2
Caldecott 21 F4
Caldercruix 34 A1
Caldicot 7 F2
Caldwell 30 C3
Calfsound 49 E2
Calgary 36 B2
Callander 38 A4
Callington 4 B2
Calne 14 B4
Calver 20 C1
Calverton 21 E2
Calvine 38 B2
Cam 14 A3
Camasnacroise 37 D2
Camberley 9 F1
Camberwell 51 E4
Camborne 3 E3
Cambridge 16 B2
Cambridge Airport 16 B2
Camelford 4 A2
Camer 51 H5
Campbeltown 32 C3
Camptown 35 D4
Camrose 12 A1
Cannich 41 E3
Cannington 7 E3
Cannock 20 B3
Canonbie 29 F1
Canterbury 11 E2
Canton 7 E2
Canvey Island 11 D1
Canwell Hall 53 D1
Caolas 36 A2
Caolas Scalpaigh 47 E3
Capel 10 B3
Capel Curig 18 C2
Capel St. Mary 17 D2
Cappercleuch 34 B3
Capplegill 34 B4
Caputh 38 C3
Carbost (Loch Harport)
  High. 40 B3
Carbost (Loch Snizort
  Beag) *High.* 40 B3
Carcroft 26 B3
Cardenden 39 D4
Cardiff 7 E2
Cardiff International
  Airport 7 D2
Cardigan 12 A3
Cardross 33 E1
Cargenbridge 29 D1

Cargill 38 C3
Carlabhagh 47 E1
Carlisle 29 F2
Carlops 34 B2
Carlton *Leics.* 53 F1
Carlton *Notts.* 21 E2
Carlton Colville 23 F4
Carlton in Lindrick 26 B4
Carlton-on-Trent 21 E1
Carluke 34 A2
Carmarthen 12 B4
Carmyllie 39 E3
Carnbee 39 E4
Carnbo 38 C4
Carnforth 24 C1
Carno 13 D1
Carnoustie 39 E3
Carnwath 34 A2
Carradale 32 C3
Carrbridge 42 B4
Carronbridge 34 A4
Carsaig 36 C3
Carshalton 50 D5
Carsluith 28 C2
Carsphairn 33 F4
Carstairs 34 A2
Carterton 14 C3
Cartmel 24 C1
Castle Bromwich 20 C4
Castle Bromwich 53 D3
Castle Carrock 30 A2
Castle Cary 8 A2
Castle Donnington 21 D3
Castle Douglas 29 D2
Castle End 53 E4
Castle Kennedy 28 A2
Castlebay (Bagh a
  Chaisteil) 46 A4
Castleford 26 A3
Castlemartin 12 A2
Castleside 30 C2
Castleton *N.Yorks.* 31 E4
Castletown *High.* 45 E1
Castletown *I.o.M.* 24 A3
Caterham 10 B2
Catford 51 E4
Caton 25 D1
Catrine 33 F3
Catshill 14 B1
Catshill 52 B4
Catterick 30 C4
Catterick Camp 30 C4
Caunsall 52 A3
Caverswall 20 B2
Cawdor 42 A2
Cawood 26 B2
Cawston 23 E3
Caythorpe 21 F2
Cayton 27 D1
Ceann a'Bháigh 46 A1
Cearsiadar 47 E2
Cefn-mawr 19 E2
Ceres 39 D4
Cerrigydrudion 19 D2
Chad Valley 52 C3
Chadderton 25 E4
**Chaddesley Corbett
  52 A4**
**Chadwell St. Mary
  51 H4**
Chadwick End 53 E4
Chagford 4 C1
Chailey 10 B3
Chalfont Common 50 B2
Chalfont St. Giles 10 A1
Chalfont St. Giles 50 A2
Chalfont St. Peter 50 B2

Chalford 14 B3
Chalgrove 15 E4
Champany 34 A1
Chalk 51 H4
Chandler's Cross 50 B2
Chapel End 53 F2
Chapel Fields 53 F4
Chapel St. Leonards
  22 B1
Chapel-en-le-Frith 25 F4
Chapelhall 34 A2
Chapeltown *S.Yorks.*
  26 A4
Chard 5 F1
Chardstock 5 F1
Charfield 14 A4
Charing 11 E2
Charlbury 15 D3
Charlestown 43 F4
Charlesworth 25 E4
Charlton *Gt.Lon.* 51 F4
Charlton *Hants.* 9 D1
Charlton *Wilts.* 14 B4
Charlton Kings 14 B3
Charlwood 10 B3
Charminster 8 A3
Charmouth 5 F1
Chartham 11 E2
Chartridge 50 A1
Chasetown 52 C1
Chatham 11 D2
Chatteris 22 B4
Chatton 35 E3
Cheadle *Gt.Man.* 25 E4
Cheadle *Staffs.* 20 B2
Cheam 50 D5
Cheapside 50 A5
Checkley *Staffs.* 20 B2
Chedburgh 16 C2
Cheddar 7 F3
Cheddleton 20 B2
Chelmorton 20 C1
Chelmsford 16 C3
Chelsfield 51 F5
Cheltenham 14 B3
Chenies 50 B2
Chepstow 7 F1
Cheriton 9 E2
Chertsey 10 A2
Chertsey 50 B5
Chesham 15 F3
Chesham 50 A1
Chesham Bois 50 A2
Cheshunt 16 B4
Cheshunt 51 E1
Cheslyn Hay 52 B1
Chessington 50 C5
Chester 19 F2
Chester-le-Street 31 D2
Chesterfield *Derbys.*
  21 D1
**Chesterfield *Staffs.*
  53 D1**
Chesters 35 D4
Chew Magna 8 A1
Chichester 9 F3
Chickerell 8 A4
Chiddingfold 9 F2
Chieveley 15 D4
**Chignall St. James
  51 H1**
Chigwell 10 C1
Chigwell 51 F2
Chigwell Row 51 F2
Chilcompton 8 A1
Childerditch 51 H3
Childrey 15 D4

Chilham 11 E2
Chilton 31 D3
Chilvers Coton 53 F2
Chingford 10 B1
Chingford 51 E2
Chinnor 15 E3
Chippenham 14 B4
Chipperfield 50 B1
Chipping Campden
  14 C2
Chipping Norton 14 C2
Chipping Ongar 16 B4
Chipping Ongar 51 G1
Chipping Sodbury 14 A4
Chirbury 13 E1
Chirk 19 E3
Chirnside 35 E2
Chiseldon 14 C4
Chislehurst 51 F4
Chiswell Green 50 C1
Chiswick 50 D4
Chobham 50 A5
Cholesbury 50 A1
Chopwell 30 C2
Chorley 25 D3
Chorleywood 15 F4
Chorleywood 50 B2
Christchurch *Dorset*
  8 C4
Christon Bank 35 F3
Chryston 33 F1
Chudleigh 5 D2
Chulmleigh 6 C4
Church Aston 20 A3
**Church End *Warks.*
  53 E2**
Church Lawton 20 B1
Church Stretton 13 F1
Churchdown 14 B3
Churchgate 51 E1
Churchill *Worcs.* 52 A4
Cilcain 19 E2
Cille Bhrighde 46 A3
Cinderford 14 A3
Cirencester 14 B3
City of London 51 E4
**City of Westminster
  50 D3**
Clabhach 36 A2
Clachan (Kintyre)
  Arg. & B. 32 C2
Clachan (Loch Fyne)
  Arg. & B. 37 E4
Clachan (Raasay) *High.*
  40 B3
Clachan of Glendaruel
  33 D1
Clachtoll 44 A3
Clackmannan 34 A1
Clacton-on-Sea 17 E3
Cladich 37 D2
Claggan 37 D2
Clanfield *Oxon.* 14 C3
Claonaig 32 C2
Clapham *Beds.* 15 F1
Clapham *Gt.Lon.* 50 D4
Clapham *N.Yorks.* 25 D1
Clarborough 26 B4
Clare 16 C2
Clashmore 42 A1
Clashnessie 44 A3
Clatt 42 C4
Clatterford End 51 G1
Clavering 16 B3
Claverton 53 D5
Clay Cross 21 D1
Claydon 17 E2
Claygate *Surr.* 50 C5

**Clayhanger *W.Mid.*
  52 C1**
Claypole 21 F2
Clayton *W.Suss.* 10 B4
Clayton West 25 F3
Clayton-le-Moors 25 D3
Clayton-le-Woods 25 D3
Cleadale 36 C1
Cleadon 31 D1
Cleat 49 E4
Cleator Moor 29 E3
Cleckheaton 25 F3
Cleehill 14 A1
Cleethorpes 27 E3
Clehonger 13 F4
Cleland 34 A2
Clenchwarton 22 B3
Clent 20 B4
Clent 52 B4
Cleobury Mortimer
  14 A1
Clestrain 49 D3
Clevedon 7 F2
Cleveleys 24 C2
Clewer Village 50 A4
Cliffe 11 D1
Cliffe Woods 11 D1
Clipstone 21 E1
Clitheroe 25 D2
Closeburn 34 A4
Cloughton 31 F4
Clova 39 D1
Clovelly 6 B4
Clovenfords 34 C3
Clovullin 37 E2
Clowne 21 D1
Clun 13 E2
Clunes 37 E1
Clutton 8 A1
Clydach 6 C1
Clydach Vale 7 D1
Clydebank 33 F1
Clynderwen 12 A4
Clyro 13 E3
Coalburn 34 A3
Coalville 21 D3
Coast 41 D1
Coatbridge 33 F2
Cobham *Kent* 51 H5
Cobham *Surr.* 10 A2
Cock Bridge 42 C4
Cockburnspath 35 D1
Cockenzie & Port Seton
  34 C1
Cockerham 24 C2
Cockermouth 29 E3
Cockett 6 C1
Cockfield 30 C3
Cockfosters 50 D2
Coddenham 17 E2
Coddington 21 F1
Codicote 16 A3
Codnor 21 D2
Codsall 20 B3
Codsall 52 A1
Codsall Wood 52 A1
Cofton Hackett 52 C4
Coggeshall 17 D3
Colchester 17 D3
Coldblow 51 G4
Colden Common 9 E2
Coldingham 35 E2
Coldstream 35 E3
Coleford 14 A3
Colehill 8 C3
Coleshill *Bucks.* 50 A2
Coleshill *Warks.* 20 C4

Coleshill *Warks.* 53 E3
Colintraive 33 D1
Collafirth 48 B2
Collier Row 51 G2
Collieston 43 F3
Collin 29 E1
Collingham 21 F1
Collycroft 53 F3
Colmonell 28 A1
Colnabaichin 42 C4
Colnbrook 10 A1
Colnbrook 50 B4
Colne 25 E2
Colney Heath 16 A4
Colney Heath 50 D1
Colney Street 50 C1
Colquhar 34 C2
Colsterworth 21 F3
Coltishall 23 E3
Colwich 20 B3
Colwick 21 E2
Colwyn Bay 18 C1
Colyford 5 E1
Colyton 5 E1
Combe Martin 6 C3
Combe St. Nicholas 7 E4
Comberford 53 D1
Comberton 16 B2
Comrie 38 B3
Congdon's Shop 4 B2
Congerstone 53 F1
Congleton 20 B1
Congresbury 7 F2
Coningsby 22 A2
Conisbrough 26 A4
Coniston 29 F4
Connah's Quay 19 E1
Connel 37 D3
Conon Bridge 41 F2
Consett 30 C2
Constantine 3 E3
Contin 41 F2
Conwy 18 C1
Cookham 15 F4
Cookley *Worcs.* 20 B4
Cookley *Worcs.* **52 A3**
Cooksmill Green 51 H1
Coombe Bissett 8 C2
Cooper's Hill 50 A4
**Coopersale Common
51 F1**
Copley 30 C3
Copplestone 5 D1
Coppull 25 D3
Copt Heath 53 D4
Copythorne 9 D3
Corbridge 30 B1
Corby 21 F4
Corfe Castle 8 C4
Corfe Mullen 8 C3
Corley 53 E3
Corley Ash 53 E3
Corley Moor 53 E3
Cornhill 43 D2
Cornhill-on-Tweed 35 E3
Cornholme 25 E3
Corpach 37 E1
Corrie 33 D3
Corringham 11 D1
Corsham 8 B1
Corsock 29 D1
Corton 23 F4
Corwen 19 D2
Coryton 11 D1
Cosby 21 D4
Coseley 52 B2
Coshieville 38 B2

Cotgrave 21 E2
Coton *Staffs.* **53 D1**
Cottenham 16 B1
Cotteridge 52 C3
Cottesmore 21 F3
Cottingham *E.Riding*
27 D2
Cottingham *Northants.*
21 F4
Coulport 33 E1
Coundon 30 C3
Coupar Angus 39 D3
**Court House Green
53 F3**
Cove *Arg. & B.* 33 E1
Cove *High.* 40 C1
Cove Bay 43 F4
Coven 52 B1
Coventry 21 D4
Coventry 53 F4
Coventry Airport 53 F4
Coverack 3 F4
Cowbit 22 A3
Cowbridge 7 D2
Cowdenbeath 34 B1
Cowes 9 E3
Cowfold 10 B3
Cowie 34 A1
Cowley *Gt.Lon.* **50 B3**
Cowling 25 E2
Cowshill 30 B2
Coxheath 11 D2
Coxtie Green 51 G2
Coxwold 26 B1
Coychurch 7 D2
Coylton 33 E3
Coylumbridge 42 B4
Crabbs Cross 52 C5
Cradley *Here.* 14 A2
Cradley *W.Mid.* **52 B3**
Craichie 39 E2
Craig 41 D3
Craigandaive 33 D1
Craigdarroch 33 F4
Craigellachie 42 C3
Craigendoran 33 E1
Craighat 33 F1
Craignure 37 D3
Crail 39 E4
Cramlington 31 D1
Cramond 34 B1
Cranage 20 A1
Cranbourne 50 A4
Cranfield 15 F2
Cranford *Gt.Lon.* **50 C4**
Cranham *Gt.Lon.* **51 G3**
Cranleigh 10 A3
Cranshaws 35 D2
Cranwell 21 F2
Crask Inn 44 C3
Craster 35 F3
Crathie 39 D1
Craven Arms 13 F2
Crawfordjohn 34 A3
Crawley 10 B3
Crayford 51 G4
Creag Ghoraidh 46 B2
Credenhill 13 F3
Crediton 5 D1
Creekmouth 51 F3
Creetown 28 C2
Cregneash 24 A3
Creswell 21 D1
Crewe 20 A1
Crewkerne 5 F1
Crianlarich 37 F3
Criccieth 18 B3

Crickhowell 13 E4
Cricklade 14 C4
Crieff 38 B3
Crigglestone 26 A3
Crimond 43 F2
Crinan 37 D4
Cringleford 23 E4
Cripp's Corner 11 D3
Crockenhill 51 G5
Crocketford or Ninemile
Bar 29 D1
Croeserw 7 D1
Crofton 26 A3
Crofty 6 B1
Cromarty 42 A2
Cromer 23 E2
Cromford 20 C1
Cromhall 14 A4
Crondall 9 F1
Crook 30 C3
Crookham 35 E3
Crosbost 47 E2
Crosby *Mersey.* 24 C4
Crosby *N.Lincs.* 26 C3
Crosby Ravensworth 30 A3
Cross Inn 12 C3
Crossaig 32 C2
Crosscanonby 29 E2
Crossford *Fife* 34 B1
Crossford *S.Lan.* 34 A2
Crossgates *Fife* 34 B1
Crossgates *Powys* 13 E3
Crosshands 33 F3
Crosshill 33 E4
Crosshouse 33 E3
Crossmichael 28 C1
Crossway 13 D3
Crossway Green 52 A5
Croston 24 C3
Croughton 15 D2
Crow Hill 14 A2
Crowborough 10 C3
Crowland 22 A3
Crowle 26 C3
Crowthorne 9 F1
Croxley Green 50 B2
Croy *High.* 42 A3
Croy *N.Lan.* 33 F1
Croyde 6 B3
Croydon *Gt.Lon.* **51 E5**
Cruden Bay 43 F3
Crulabhig 47 E2
Crumlin 7 E1
Crymych 12 A4
Crynant 6 C1
Crystal Palace 51 E4
Cubbington 15 D1
Cubbington 53 F5
Cuckfield 10 B3
Cuddington *Ches.* 19 F1
Cudworth 26 A3
Cuffley 51 E1
Cuffley 16 A4
Culbokie 41 F2
Culcheth 19 F1
Culdrain 43 D3
Cullen 43 D2
Cullicudden 42 A2
Cullingworth 25 F2
Cullipool 37 D4
Cullivoe 48 C1
Cullompton 5 E1
Culnacraig 44 A4
Culnaknock 40 B2
Culross 34 A1
Culswick 48 B3

Cults 43 E4
**Culverstone Green
51 H5**
Cumbernauld 34 A1
Cuminestown 43 E2
Cumnock 33 F3
Cumnor 15 D3
Cunningsburgh 48 B4
Cupar 39 E4
Curdworth 53 D2
Curry Rivel 7 F4
Cutnall Green 52 A5
Cwm 7 E1
Cwmafan 6 C1
Cwmbran 7 E1
Cwmllynfell 6 C1
Cydwelli (Kidwelly) 6 B1
Cymmer 7 D1
Cynghordy 13 D4
Cynwyl Elfed 12 B4

D

Dacre 29 F3
Dagenham 51 F3
Dail Bho Thuath 47 F1
Dailly 33 E4
Dairsie 39 D4
Dalabrog 46 A3
Dalbeattie 29 D2
Dalby 24 A3
Dale *Pembs.* 12 A2
Dalgety Bay 34 B1
Dalham 16 C1
Dalkeith 34 C2
Dallas 42 B2
Dalmally 37 E3
Dalmellington 33 F4
Dalnavie 42 A2
Dalry 33 E2
Dalrymple 33 E4
Dalston 29 F2
Dalton *S.Yorks.* 26 A4
Dalton-in-Furness 24 B1
Dalwhinnie 38 A1
Damerham 8 C3
Danbury 16 C4
Danby 31 E4
Danehill 10 B3
Darenth 51 G4
Darfield 26 A4
Darlaston 52 B2
Darlington 31 D3
Darra 43 E3
Dartford 10 C1
Dartford 51 G4
Dartington 5 D2
Dartmeet 4 C2
Dartmouth 5 D3
Darton 26 A3
Darvel 33 F3
Darwen 25 D3
Datchet 50 A4
Dava 42 B3
Davenham 20 A1
Daventry 15 D1
Daviot 42 A3
Dawlish 5 D2
Deal 11 F2
Dearham 29 E3
Debenham 17 E1
Dechmont 34 A1
Deddington 15 D2
Dedham 17 D2
Deeping St. James 22 A3
Deeping St. Nicholas
22 A3

Deganwy 18 C1
Delabole 4 A1
Delamere 19 F2
Denbigh 19 D2
Denby Dale 25 F3
Denham *Bucks.* 10 A1
Denham *Bucks.* **50 B3**
Denham Green 50 B3
Denholm 35 D3
Denholme 25 F2
Dennington 17 E1
Denny 34 A1
Denton 25 E4
Denver 22 C4
Deptford *Gt.Lon.* **51 E4**
Derby 21 D2
Dersingham 22 C3
Dervaig 36 C2
Desborough 21 E4
Devil's Bridge 12 C2
Devizes 8 C1
Dewsbury 25 F3
Dhoon 24 B2
Dibden 9 D3
Didcot 15 D4
Dinas Powys 7 E2
Dingwall 41 F2
Dinnet 43 D4
Dinnington *S.Yorks.*
26 B4
Dippen 32 C3
Dirleton 34 C1
Diss 17 E1
Distington 29 E3
Ditton *Kent* 11 D2
Dobwalls 4 A2
Dochgarroch 41 F3
Docking 22 C2
Doddinghurst 51 G2
Doddington 35 E3
Dodford *Worcs.* **52 B4**
Dodington 14 A4
Dodworth 26 A4
Dogdyke 22 A2
Dolanog 13 E1
Dolbenmaen 18 B3
Dolfor 13 E2
Dolgarrog 18 C2
Dolgellau 12 C1
Dollar 38 B4
Dolphinton 34 B2
Doncaster 26 B4
Donington 22 A2
Donkey Town 50 A5
Donnington *Tel. & W.*
20 A3
Dorchester 8 A4
Dordon 20 C4
Dordon 53 E1
Dores 41 F3
Dorking 10 B2
Dorney 50 A4
Dornie 41 D3
Dornoch 42 A1
Dorridge 53 D4
Dosthill 53 E1
Dougarie 32 C3
Douglas *I.o.M.* 24 B3
Douglas *S.Lan.* 34 A3
Douglastown 39 D2
Dounby 49 D3
Doune 38 B4
Dounreay 45 E1
Dover 11 F3
Doverdale 52 A5
Doveridge 20 C2

Dowally 38 C2
Downe 51 F5
Downham Market 22 C4
Downton 8 C2
Dowsby 22 A3
Drakes Cross 52 C4
Drayton Worcs. 52 B4
Drayton Norf. 23 E3
Drayton Oxon. 15 D4
Drayton Bassett 53 D1
Drefach 6 B1
Dreghorn 33 E3
Drem 34 C1
Driffield 27 D2
Drimnin 36 C2
Droitwich 14 B1
Droitwich 52 A5
Dronfield 21 D1
Drongan 33 F3
Dropmore 50 A3
Droylsden 25 E4
Druid 19 D3
Druimdrishaig 32 C1
Drumbeg 44 A3
Drumclog 33 F3
Drumlithie 39 F1
Drummore 28 A2
Drumnadrochit 41 F3
Drybrook 14 A3
Drymen 33 F1
Duddo 35 E2
Dudley W.Mid. 20 B4
Dudley W.Mid. 52 B2
Dudley Port 52 B2
Duffield 21 D2
Dufftown 42 C3
Duirinish 40 C3
Dullingham 16 C2
Dulnain Bridge 42 B3
Dulverton 7 D4
Dulwich 51 E4
Dumbarton 33 E1
Dumfries 29 D1
Dunbar 35 D1
Dunbeath 45 E3
Dunblane 38 B4
Dunchurch 15 D1
Dundee 39 D3
Dundonald 33 E3
Dundreggan 41 E4
Dundrennan 29 D2
Dunecht 43 E4
Dunfermline 34 B1
Dunhampton 52 A5
Dunholme 21 F1
Dunkeld 38 C3
Dunkirk 11 E2
Dunlop 33 E2
Dunnet 45 E1
Dunning 38 C4
Dunoon 33 D1
Dunragit 28 A2
Duns 35 D2
Dunscore 29 D1
Dunstable 15 F3
Dunster 7 D3
Dunton Wayletts 51 H3
Dunure 33 E4
Dunvant 6 C1
Dunvegan 40 A3
Durham 31 D2
Durness 44 B1
Durrington 8 C1
Dursley 14 A3
Dyce 43 E4
Dyke 42 B2
Dykehead 39 D2

Dymchurch 11 E3
Dymock 14 A2
Dyserth 19 D1

E
Eaglescliffe 31 D3
Eaglesfield 29 E1
Eaglesham 33 F2
Ealing 50 C3
Earby 25 E2
Eardisley 13 E3
Earith 16 B1
Earl Shilton 21 D4
Earl Stonham 17 E2
Earls Barton 15 F1
Earls Colne 17 D3
Earlsdon 53 F4
Earlston 35 D3
Earlswood Warks. 53 D4
Earsairidh 46 A4
Easdale 37 D4
Easebourne 9 F2
Easington Dur. 31 D2
Easington E.Riding
27 E3
Easington Colliery 31 D2
Easingwold 26 B1
East Barnet 50 D2
East Bedfont 50 B4
East Bergholt 17 D2
East Bridgford 21 E2
East Calder 34 B1
East Dereham 23 D3
East Goscote 21 E3
East Grinstead 10 B3
East Ham 51 F3
East Hanney 15 D4
East Harling 23 D4
East Haven 39 E3
East Horndon 51 H3
East Horsley 10 A2
East Huntspill 7 F3
East Keal 22 B1
East Kilbride 33 F2
East Leake 21 D3
East Linton 35 D1
East Malling 11 D2
East Markham 21 E1
East Midlands
International Airport
21 D2
East Molesey 50 C5
East Preston 10 A4
East Retford (Retford)
21 E1
East Wemyss 39 D4
East Wickham 51 F4
East Wittering 9 F3
Eastbourne E.Suss.
10 C4
Eastbury Herts. 50 C2
Eastcote Gt.Lon. 50 C3
Eastcote W.Mid. 53 D4
Easter Lednathie 39 D2
Easter Quarff 48 B4
Eastfield 27 D1
Eastgate 30 B2
Eastleigh Hants. 9 D3
Eastoft 26 C3
Easton 8 A4
Easton on the Hill 21 F3
Easton-in-Gordano 7 F2
Eastriggs 29 F1
Eastry 11 F2
Eastwood Notts. 21 D2
Eathorpe 53 F5

Eaton Socon 16 A1
Ebbw Vale 7 E1
Ecclaw 35 D1
Ecclefechan 29 E1
Eccles Sc.Bord. 35 D2
Ecclesfield 26 A4
Eccleshall 20 B2
Eccleston Lancs. 25 D3
Echt 43 E4
Eckford 35 D3
Eckington Derbys. 21 D1
Eckington Worcs. 14 B2
Edderton 42 A1
Eddleston 34 B2
Eden Park 51 E5
Edenbridge 10 C2
Edenfield 25 E3
Edgbaston 52 C3
Edgware 50 D2
Edgworth 25 D3
Edial 52 C1
Edinburgh 34 B1
Edinburgh Airport 34 B1
Edlingham 35 F4
Edmonton 51 E2
Edmundbyers 30 C2
Edney Common 51 H1
Edstone 53 D5
Edwinstowe 21 E1
Edzell 39 E2
Egglescliffe 31 D3
Egham 10 A1
Egham 50 B4
Eglingham 35 F3
Eglwys Fach 12 C1
Eglwyswrw 12 A4
Egremont 29 E3
Egton 31 F4
Einacleit 47 D2
Elgin 42 C2
Elgol 40 B4
Elham 11 E2
Elie 39 E4
Eling 9 D3
Elland 25 F3
Ellesmere 19 E3
Ellesmere Port 19 F1
Ellingham 35 F3
Ellington 35 F4
Ellon 43 F3
Elloughton 26 C3
Elm 22 B4
Elm Park 51 G3
Elmbridge 52 B5
Elmdon W.Mid. 53 D3
Elmdon Heath 53 D3
Elmley Lovett 52 A5
Elmswell 17 D1
Elmton 21 D1
Elphin 44 B3
Elsdon 35 E4
Elsrickle 34 B2
Elstead 9 F2
Elstree 16 A4
Elstree 50 C2
Elswick 24 C2
Eltham 51 F4
Elton Cambs. 22 A4
Elton Ches. 19 F1
Elvanfoot 34 A3
Elvington 26 B2
Ely Cambs. 16 B1
Ely Cardiff 7 E2
Embleton 35 F3
Emsworth 9 F3
Enderby 21 D4
Endon 20 B2

Enfield 51 E2
Englefield Green 50 A4
Enstone 15 D2
Enterkinfoot 34 A4
Enville 52 A3
Eoropaidh 47 F1
Epping 16 B4
Epping Green Essex
51 F1
Epping Green Herts.
50 D1
Epping Upland 51 F1
Epsom 10 B2
Epsom 50 D5
Epworth 26 C4
Erdington 53 D2
Eriboll 44 B2
Eriswell 16 C1
Erith 51 G4
Errogie 41 F4
Errol 39 D3
Esh Winning 30 C2
Esher 10 A2
Esher 50 C5
Eskdalemuir 34 B4
Essendon 50 D1
Essington 52 B1
Eston 31 E3
Eton 10 A1
Eton 50 A4
Eton Wick 50 A4
Etteridge 38 A1
Ettingshall 52 B2
Ettington 14 C2
Ettrick 34 B4
Ettrickbridge 34 C3
Euxton 25 D3
Evanton 41 F2
Evercreech 8 A2
Evesham 14 B2
Ewell 10 B2
Ewell 50 D5
Ewhurst 10 A3
Exebridge 7 D4
Exeter 5 D1
Exminster 5 D1
Exmouth 5 E2
Eye Peter. 22 A4
Eye Suff. 17 E1
Eyemouth 35 E2
Eynsford 10 C2
Eynsford 51 G5
Eynsham 15 D3

F
Failsworth 25 E4
Fair Oak Hants. 9 E3
Fairfield Worcs. 52 B4
Fairford 14 C3
Fairlie 33 E2
Fairlight 11 D4
Fairseat 51 H5
Fakenham 23 D3
Falkirk 34 A1
Falkland 39 D4
Fallin 34 A1
Falmouth 3 F3
Falstone 30 A1
Fareham 9 E3
Faringdon 14 C4
Farington 25 D3
Farleigh Surr. 51 E5
Farnborough 8 A1
Farnborough Gt.Lon.
51 F5

Farnborough Hants.
9 F1
Farndon 21 E2
Farnham 9 F1
Farnham Common 50 A3
Farnham Royal 10 A1
Farnham Royal 50 A3
Farningham 51 G5
Farnsfield 21 E1
Farnworth Gt.Man.
25 D3
Farr 42 A3
Fauldhouse 34 A2
Faversham 11 E2
Fawkham Green 51 G5
Fawley Hants. 9 D3
Fazeley 20 C4
Fazeley 53 E1
Fearnhead 19 F1
Fearnmore 40 C2
Featherstone Staffs.
20 B3
Featherstone Staffs.
52 B1
Featherstone W.Yorks.
26 A3
Felden 50 B1
Felindre 13 E2
Felixstowe 17 E2
Felling 31 D1
Felsted 16 C3
Feltham 50 C4
Felton 35 F4
Feltwell 22 C4
Fen End 53 E4
Feniton 5 E1
Fenny Drayton 53 F2
Fenstanton 16 A1
Fenwick E.Ayr. 33 F2
Fenwick Nhumb. 35 F2
Feochaig 32 C4
Feolin Ferry 32 B2
Fern 39 E2
Ferndale 7 D1
Ferndown 8 C3
Ferness 42 B3
Fernhill Heath 14 B1
Fernhurst 9 F2
Ferryden 39 E2
Ferryhill 31 D3
Feshiebridge 42 A4
Fettercairn 39 E1
Ffestiniog 18 C3
Ffostrasol 12 B3
Fiddlers Hamlet 51 F1
Filey 27 D1
Fillongley 20 C4
Fillongley 53 E3
Filton 14 A4
Fimber 26 C1
Finavon 39 E2
Finchampstead 9 F1
Finchingfield 16 C3
Finchley 50 D2
Findern 20 C2
Findhorn 42 B2
Findochty 43 D2
Findon 10 A4
Finedon 15 F1
Finningham 17 D1
Finningley 26 B4
Finnygaud 43 D2
Finsbury 51 E3
Finstall 52 B4
Finstown 49 E3
Fintry 33 F1
Fionnphort 36 B3

Fishburn 31 D3
Fishguard 12 B1
Fishnish 36 C3
Fiunary 36 C2
Flackwell Heath 15 F4
Flamborough 27 D1
Flamstead End 51 E1
Fleet 9 F1
Fleetwood 24 C2
Flempton 16 C1
Flimby 29 E3
Flimwell 11 D3
Flint 19 E1
Flitwick 15 F2
Flodden 35 E3
Flookburgh 24 C1
Fochabers 42 C2
Foleshill 53 F3
Folkestone 11 F3
Folkingham 21 F2
Folly Gate 4 C1
Foots Cray 51 F4
Ford *Arg. & B.* 37 D4
Ford *Nhumb.* 35 E3
Fordham 16 C1
Fordingbridge 8 C3
Fordoun 39 F1
Fordyce 43 D2
Forest Gate 51 F3
Forest Row 10 C3
Forfar 39 D2
Forgandenny 38 C3
Forgie 42 C2
Formby 24 C3
Forres 42 B2
Forsbrook 20 B2
Forsinard 45 D2
Fort Augustus 41 E4
Fort William 37 E1
Forth 34 A2
Fortingall 38 B2
Fortrose 42 A2
Fortuneswell 8 A4
Forty Green 50 A2
Forty Hill 51 E2
Foster Street 51 F1
Fotherby 27 E4
Foulden 35 E2
Foulridge 25 E2
Four Ashes *Staffs.*
  52 B1
Four Crosses *Staffs.*
  52 B1
Four Elms 10 C2
Four Marks 9 E2
Four Oaks *E.Suss.*
  11 D3
Four Oaks (Meriden)
  ***W.Mid.* 53 E3**
Four Oaks (Sutton
  Coldfield) *W.Mid.*
  53 D2
Fowey 4 A3
Fownhope 14 A2
Foxdale 24 A3
Foyers 41 F4
Framfield 10 C3
Framlingham 17 E1
Frampton Cotterell
  14 A4
Frampton on Severn
  14 A3
Franche 52 A4
Frankley 20 B4
Frankley 52 B3
Fraserburgh 43 F2

Freckleton 24 C3
Fremington 6 B4
Freshwater 9 D4
Freshwater East 12 B2
Fressingfield 17 E1
Freswick 45 F1
Freuchie 39 D4
Fridaythorpe 26 C1
Friern Barnet 50 D2
Frimley 9 F1
Frinton-on-Sea 17 E3
Friockheim 39 E2
Frithelstock Stone 6 B4
Frizington 29 E3
Frodsham 19 F1
Frogmore *Hants.* 9 F1
Frogmore *Herts.* **50 C1**
Frome 8 B1
Fryerning 51 H1
Fulbourn 16 B2
Fulford *Staffs.* 20 B2
Fulford *York* 26 B2
Fulham 10 B1
Fulham 50 D4
Fulmer 50 A3
Fulwood *Lancs.*
  25 D2
Funzie 48 C1
Furnace 37 E4
Fyfield *Essex* 16 B3
Fyfield *Essex* **51 G1**
Fyvie 43 E3

G

Gaer 13 E4
Gainford 30 C3
Gainsborough 26 C4
Gairloch 40 C1
Galashiels 34 C3
Galley Common 53 F2
Gallowstree Elm 52 A3
Galmisdale 36 C1
Galston 33 F3
Gamlingay 16 A2
Gardenstown 43 E2
Garderhouse 48 B3
Garelochhead 33 E1
Garforth 26 A2
Gargrave 25 E2
Garlieston 28 C2
Garsdale Head 30 B4
Garstang 24 C2
Garth 13 D3
Garthmyl 13 E1
Gartocharn 33 E1
Garvald 35 D1
Garvamore 38 A1
Garvard 32 A1
Garve 41 F2
Gatehouse of Fleet
  28 C2
Gateshead 31 D2
Gatley 25 E4
Gatwick (London) Airport
  10 B3
Gawthrop 30 A4
Gayton 22 C3
Gearraidh na h-Aibhne
  47 E2
Geddington 21 F4
Gedney 22 B3
Gelligaer 7 E1
George Green 50 B3
Georgeham 6 B3
Gerrards Cross 10 A1
Gerrards Cross 50 A3

Gidea Park 51 G3
Giffnock 33 F2
Gifford 34 C1
Gilberdyke 26 C3
Gillamoor 31 E4
Gilling West 30 C4
Gillingham *Dorset* 8 B2
Gillingham *Medway*
  11 D2
Gilmerton 38 B3
Gilsland 30 A1
Gilston 34 C2
Gilwern 7 E1
Girlsta 48 B3
Girvan 33 E4
Gisburn 25 E2
Glamis 39 D2
Glanaman 6 C1
Glanton 35 E4
Glasbury 13 E4
Glascote 53 E1
Glasgow 33 F2
Glasgow Airport 33 F2
Glassford 33 F2
Glastonbury 7 F3
Glemsford 16 C2
Glen Vine 24 A3
Glenbarr 32 B3
Glenbeg 36 C2
Glenborrodale 36 C2
Glenbreck 34 B3
Glenbrittle 40 B4
Glencaple 29 E1
Glencarse 38 C3
Glencoe 37 E2
Gleneagles 38 B4
Glenegedale 32 A2
Glenelg 40 C4
Glenfarg 38 C4
Glenfield 21 D3
Glenfinnan 37 D1
Glengarnock 33 E2
Glenkindie 43 D4
Glenluce 28 A2
Glenrothes 39 D4
Glinton 22 A4
Glossop 25 F4
Gloucester 14 B3
Glusburn 25 E2
Glyn Ceiriog 19 E3
Glyn-Neath 7 D1
Glyncorrwg 7 D1
Gnosall 20 B3
Gobowen 19 E3
Godalming 10 A2
Godmanchester 16 A1
Godstone 10 B2
Goff's Oak 51 E1
Golborne 25 D4
Goldcliff 7 F2
Golden Pot 9 F2
Golders Green 50 D3
Golspie 45 D4
Goodwick 12 A1
Goodyers End 53 F3
Goole 26 B3
Goonhavern 3 F2
Gorcott Hill 52 C5
Gordon 35 D2
Gorebridge 34 C2
Goring 15 E4
Gornalwood 52 B2
Gorseinon 6 C1
Gosberton 22 A3
Gosfield 16 C3
Gosforth *Cumb.* 29 E4
Gosforth *T. & W.* 30 C1

Gospel End 52 B2
Gosport 9 E3
Gotham 21 D2
Goudhurst 11 D3
Gourdon 39 F2
Goxhill 27 D3
Grabhair 47 E2
Grain 11 D1
Grampound 3 F3
Grandtully 38 B2
Grange Hill 51 F2
Grange-over-Sands
  24 C1
Grangemouth 34 A1
Grantham 21 F2
Grantown-on-Spey
  42 B3
Grantshouse 35 D2
Grasmere 29 F4
Grassington 25 E1
Gravelly Hill 53 D2
Gravesend 10 C1
Gravesend 51 H4
Grayrigg 30 A4
Grays 10 C1
Grays 51 H4
Grayshott 9 F2
Greasby 19 E1
Greasley 21 E3
Great Ayton 31 E3
Great Baddow 16 C3
Great Barr 52 C2
Great Barton 17 D1
Great Bircham 22 C3
Great Broughton 31 E4
Great Clifton 29 E3
Great Cornard 17 D2
Great Dunmow 16 C3
Great Eccleston 24 C2
Great Ellingham 23 D4
Great Glen 21 D3
Great Gonerby 21 F2
Great Gransden 16 A2
Great Harwood 25 D2
Great Heath 53 F3
Great Horkesley 17 D3
Great Linford 15 F2
Great Malvern 14 A2
Great Marton 24 C2
Great Missenden 15 F3
Great Oxney Green
  51 H1
Great Parndon 51 F1
Great Ponton 21 F2
Great Salkeld 30 A2
Great Sampford 16 C2
Great Sankey 19 F1
Great Shelford 16 B2
Great Torrington 6 B4
Great Wakering 11 E1
Great Warley 51 G2
Great Wyrley 20 B3
Great Wyrley 52 B1
Great Yarmouth 23 F3
Great Yeldham 16 C2
Greatham *Hants.* 9 F2
Greatstone-on-Sea 11 E3
Green Street 50 C2
Green Street Green
  Gt.Lon. **51 F5**
Green Street Green *Kent*
  51 G4
Greenford 50 C3
Greengairs 34 A1
Greenham 9 E1
Greenhead 30 A1
Greenhill *Gt.Lon.* **50 C3**
Greenhithe 51 G4

Greenigo 49 E3
Greenlaw 35 D2
Greenloaning 38 B4
Greenock 33 E1
Greenodd 24 C1
Greensted 51 G1
Greenway 12 A4
Greenwich 51 E4
Grendon *Warks.* **53 E2**
Grendon Common 53 E2
Gresford 19 E2
Gretna 29 F1
Greystoke 29 F3
Griais 47 F1
Griff 53 F3
Grimoldby 22 B1
Grimsby 27 D3
Grimston 22 C3
Gringley on the Hill
  26 B4
Gritley 49 E3
Grizebeck 29 E4
Grove 15 D4
Grove Park 51 F4
Grudie 41 E2
Grutness 48 B4
Guide Post 30 C1
Guildford 10 A2
Guildtown 38 C3
Guisborough 31 E3
Guiseley 25 F2
Guist 23 D3
Gullane 34 C1
Gunness 26 C3
Gunnislake 4 B2
Gurnos 6 C1
Gutcher 48 C1
Gwaun-Cae-Gurwen
  6 C1
Gwithian 3 E3
Gwytherin 18 C2

H

Hackleton 15 E1
Hacklinge 11 F2
Hackness 31 F4
Hackney 51 E3
Haddenham 16 B1
Haddington 34 C1
Haddiscoe 23 F4
Hademore 53 D1
Hadleigh 17 D2
Hadley 20 A3
Hadley Wood 50 D2
Hadzor 52 B5
Hagley *Here.* 14 A2
Hagley *Worcs.* 20 B4
Hagley *Worcs.* **52 B3**
Hailsham 10 C4
Hainault 51 F2
Hale *Gt.Man.* 25 E4
Hales 23 F4
Halesowen 20 B4
Halesowen 52 B3
Halesworth 17 F1
Halewood 19 F1
Halfpenny Green 52 A2
Halifax 25 F3
Halkirk 45 E2
Halkyn 19 E1
Hall 33 E2
Hall Green 53 D3
Halland 10 C4
Hallow 14 B1
Hallworthy 4 A1
Halstead *Essex* 16 C3

Halstead *Kent* 51 F5
Halton Gill 25 E1
Haltwhistle 30 A1
Halwell 5 D3
Ham *Gt.Lon.* **50 C4**
Ham *Shet.* 48 A3
Ham Green *Worcs.*
52 C5
Hamble-le-Rice 9 E3
Hambleton 24 C2
Hamilton 33 F2
Hammersmith & Fulham
50 C4
Hammerwich 52 C1
Hammond Street 51 E1
Hamnavoe (Mainland)
Shet. 48 B4
Hamnavoe (Yell) *Shet.*
48 C2
Hampreston 8 C3
Hampstead 50 D3
Hampton *Gt.Lon.* **50 C5**
Hampton in Arden 53 E3
Hampton Lovett 52 A5
Hampton on the Hill
53 E5
Hamstead *W.Mid.* **52 C2**
Hamstreet 11 E3
Hanbury *Worcs.* **52 B5**
Handsacre 20 C3
Handsworth *W.Mid.*
52 C2
Hanham 14 A4
Hanley Castle 14 B2
Hanwell *Gt.Lon.* **50 C4**
Hanwood 13 F1
Hanworth *Gt.Lon.* **50 C4**
Happisburgh 23 F3
Harbledown 11 E2
Harborne 52 C3
Harbury 15 D1
Hardingstone 15 E1
Hardwicke 14 A3
Hare Street 16 B3
Harefield 10 A1
Harefield 50 B2
Harewood 26 A2
Haringey 51 E3
Harlech 18 B3
Harlesden 50 D3
Harleston 23 E4
Harlington 15 F2
Harlow 16 B3
Harmondsworth 50 B4
Harmston 21 F1
Harold Hill 51 G2
Harold Wood 51 G2
Haroldswick 48 C1
Harpenden 16 A3
Harpole 15 E1
Harrietfield 38 C3
Harrietsham 11 D2
Harrogate 26 A2
Harrow *Gt.Lon.* **50 C3**
Harrow on the Hill 50 C3
Harrow Weald 50 C2
Harston 16 B2
Hartfield 10 C3
Harthill *N.Lan.* 34 A2
Hartland 6 A4
Hartlebury 14 B1
Hartlebury 52 A4
Hartlepool 31 E3
Hartley *Kent* 10 C2
Hartley *Kent* **51 H5**
Hartley Wintney 9 F1
Hartpury 14 A2

Hartshill 21 D4
Hartshill 53 F2
Hartshorne 21 D3
Harvel 51 H5
Harvington *Worcs.*
14 B2
Harvington *Worcs.*
52 A4
Harwell 15 D4
Harwich 17 E3
Harworth 26 B4
Hasbury 52 B3
Haseley 53 E5
Hasland 21 D1
Haslemere 9 F2
Haslingden 25 E3
Hassendean 34 C3
Hastings 11 D4
Hastingwood 51 F1
Hastoe 50 A1
Haswell 31 D2
Hatch End 50 C2
Hatfield *Herts.* 16 A3
Hatfield *Herts.* **50 D1**
Hatfield *S.Yorks.* 26 B3
Hatfield Broad Oak 16 B3
Hatfield Peverel 16 C3
Hatherleigh 4 C1
Hathern 21 D3
Hathersage 25 F4
Hatton *Aber.* 43 F3
Hatton *Derbys.* 20 C2
Hatton *Gt.Lon.* **50 B4**
Hatton *Warks.* **53 E5**
Haugh of Urr 29 D1
Haughton 20 B3
Havant 9 F3
Haverfordwest 12 A2
Haverhill 16 C2
Havering 51 G3
Havering-atte-Bower
51 G2
Hawarden 19 E2
Hawes 30 B4
Hawick 34 C3
Hawkes End 53 F3
Hawkhurst 11 D3
Hawkinge 11 F3
Hawkshead 29 F4
Hawkwell 11 D1
Hawley *Hants.* 9 F1
Hawley *Kent* **51 G4**
Haworth 25 F2
Haxby 26 B1
Haxey 26 C4
Hay Mills 53 D3
Hay-on-Wye 13 E3
Haydock 25 D4
Haydon Bridge 30 B1
Haydon Wick 14 C4
Hayes (Bromley) *Gt.Lon.*
51 F5
Hayes (Hillingdon)
Gt.Lon. **50 B3**
Hayfield 25 F4
Hayle 3 E3
Hayton 26 C2
Haywards Heath 10 B3
Hazel Grove 25 E4
Hazelwood *Gt.Lon.*
51 F5
Hazlemere 15 F4
Heacham 22 C2
Headcorn 11 D2
Headless Cross 52 C5
Headley 9 F2
Healeyfield 30 C2

Healing 27 D3
Heanor 21 D2
Heath 21 D1
Heath Town 52 B2
Heathfield 10 C3
Heathton 52 A2
Hebburn 31 D1
Hebden Bridge 25 E3
Heckington 22 A2
Hedge End 9 E3
Hedgerley 50 A3
Hedon 27 D3
Heglibister 48 B3
Heighington 21 F1
Helensburgh 33 E1
Helhoughton 23 D3
Hellifield 25 E2
Helmsdale 45 E3
Helmsley 31 E4
Helpringham 22 A2
Helsby 19 F1
Helston 3 E3
Hemel Hempstead 16 A3
Hemel Hempstead 50 B1
Hemingford Grey 16 A1
Hempnall 23 E4
Hempstead 16 C2
Hemsby 23 F3
Hemsworth 26 A3
Hemyock 7 E4
Hendon *Gt.Lon.* 10 B1
Hendon *Gt.Lon.* **50 D3**
Henfield 10 B4
Hengoed 7 E1
Henley-in-Arden 14 C1
Henley-in-Arden 53 D5
Henley-on-Thames 15 E4
Henlow 16 A2
Henstridge 8 B2
Hereford 13 F4
Heriot 34 C2
Herne Bay 11 E2
Herongate 51 H2
Heronsgate 50 B2
Hersham *Surr.* **50 C5**
Herstmonceux 10 C4
Herston 49 E4
Hertford 16 B3
Heston 50 C4
Heswall 19 E1
Hethersett 23 E4
Hetton 25 E1
Hetton-le-Hole 31 D2
Hewell Grange 52 C5
Hewell Lane 52 C5
Hexham 30 B1
Hextable 10 C1
Hextable 51 G4
Heybridge (Ingatestone)
Essex **51 H2**
Heybridge (Maldon)
Essex 17 D3
Heysham 24 C1
Heywood 25 E3
Hibaldstow 26 C4
High Beach 51 F2
High Bentham 25 D1
High Blantyre 33 F2
High Bradfield 26 A4
High Etherley 30 C3
High Garrett 16 C3
High Halden 11 D3
High Hawsker 31 F4
High Hesket 29 F2
High Laver 51 G1
High Legh 25 D4
High Lorton 29 E3

High Ongar 51 G1
High Wycombe 15 F4
Higham 11 D1
Higham Ferrers 15 F1
Higham on the Hill 53 F2
Highampton 4 B1
Highbridge 7 F3
Highclere 9 D1
Higher Walton *Lancs.*
25 D3
Highley 20 A4
Highnam 14 A3
Highworth 14 C4
Hildenborough 10 C2
Hilgay 22 C4
Hill End 38 C4
Hill of Fearn 42 A1
Hillingdon 50 B3
Hillside *Angus* 39 E2
Hillside *Shet.* 48 B2
Hillswick 48 B2
Hilperton 8 B1
Hilton *Derbys.* 20 C2
Himley 52 A2
Hinckley 21 D4
Hinderwell 31 F3
Hindhead 9 F2
Hindley 25 D4
Hindon 8 B2
Hingham 23 D4
Hints *Staffs.* **53 D1**
Hirwaun 7 D1
Histon 16 B1
Hitchin 16 A3
Hither Green 51 E4
Hockley 11 D1
Hockley Heath 14 C1
Hockley Heath 53 D4
Hoddesdon 16 B3
Hoddesdon 51 E1
Hodnet 19 F3
Hogsthorpe 22 B1
Holbeach 22 B3
Holbrook *Suff.* 17 E2
Holden 25 E2
Holland-on-Sea 17 E3
Hollington 11 D4
Hollingworth 25 F4
Hollybush *E.Ayr.* 33 E4
Hollybush *Worcs.* 14 A2
Holme-on-Spalding-Moor
26 C2
Holmes Chapel 20 A1
Holmesfield 20 C1
Holmfirth 25 F3
Holsworthy 4 B1
Holt *Worcs.* **52 A5**
Holt *Norf.* 23 D2
Holt *Wilts.* 8 B1
Holt *Worc.* 19 F2
Holt End *Worcs.* **52 C5**
Holt Fleet 52 A5
Holt Heath *Worcs.*
52 A5
Holtspur 50 A2
Holy Cross 52 B4
Holyhead 18 A1
Holywell 19 E1
Holywood 29 D1
Homersfield 23 E4
Honiley 53 E4
Honiton 5 E1
Honley 25 F3
Hoo 11 D1
Hook *E.Riding* 26 B3
Hook *Gt.Lon.* **50 C5**
Hook *Hants.* 9 F1

Hook Green (Meopham)
Kent **51 H5**
Hook Green (Southfleet)
Kent **51 H4**
Hook Norton 15 D2
Hope 19 E2
Hopeman 42 B2
Hopton *Norf.* 23 F4
Hopton *Suff.* 17 D1
Hopwas 53 D1
Hopwood 52 C4
Horam 10 C3
Horbling 22 A3
Horbury 26 A3
Horden 31 D2
Horeb 12 B3
Horley 10 B2
Horn Hill 50 B2
Hornby 25 D1
Horncastle 22 A1
Hornchurch 51 G3
Horndean *Hants.* 9 E3
Horndon on the Hill
51 H3
Horning 23 E3
Hornsea 27 D2
Hornsey 51 E3
Horrabridge 4 C2
Horringer 16 C1
Horsehouse 25 F1
Horsford 23 E3
Horsforth 25 F2
Horsham 10 B3
Horsmonden 11 D3
Horstead 23 E3
Horton *W. & M.* **50 B4**
Horton Heath 9 E3
Horton in Ribblesdale
25 E1
Horton Kirby 51 G5
Horwich 25 D3
Houbie 48 C1
Houghton le Spring
31 D2
Houghton Regis 15 F2
Houndslow 35 D2
Hounslow 50 C4
Houston 33 E2
Houton 49 E3
Hove 10 B4
Hoveton 23 E3
Hovingham 26 B1
Howden 26 B3
Howwood 33 E2
Hoylake 19 E1
Hoyland 26 A4
Hucknall 21 D2
Huddersfield 25 F3
Huggate 26 C2
Huish Episcopi 7 F4
Huisinis 47 D3
Hullavington 14 B4
Hullbridge 11 D1
Humberside International
Airport 27 D3
Humberston 27 E4
Humbie 34 C2
Hundleby 22 B1
Hundleton 12 A2
Hungerford 9 D1
Hunmanby 27 D1
Hunningham 53 F5
Hunstanton 22 C2
Hunt End 52 C5
Hunter's Quay 33 E1
Huntingdon 16 A1
Huntly 43 D3

Huntonbridge 50 B1
Hurley *Warks.* **53 E2**
Hurlford 33 F3
Hursley 9 D2
Hurst Green 11 D3
Hurstbourne Tarrant
　9 D1
Hurstpierpoint 10 B3
Hurworth-on-Tees 31 D3
Husbands Bosworth
　21 E4
Huttoft 22 B1
Hutton *Essex* **51 H2**
Hutton Cranswick 27 D2
Hutton Rudby 31 D4
Huyton 19 F1
Hyde 25 E4
Hyde Heath 50 A1
Hythe *Hants.* 9 D3
Hythe *Kent* 11 E3
Hythe End 50 B4

I

Ibstock 21 D3
Ickenham 50 B3
Icklesham 11 D4
Icklingham 16 C1
Idrigil 40 B2
Ifield or Singlewell
　51 H4
Ilchester 7 F4
Ilford 10 C1
Ilford 51 F3
Ilfracombe 6 B3
Ilkeston 21 D2
Ilkley 25 F2
Illey 52 B3
Ilminster 7 F4
Immingham 27 D3
Inchbare 39 E2
Inchnadamph 44 B3
Inchture 39 D3
Ingatestone 16 C4
Ingatestone 51 H1
Ingleton *Dur.* 30 C3
Ingleton *N.Yorks.*
　25 D1
Inglewhite 25 D2
Ingoldmells 22 B1
Ingrave 51 H2
Inkberrow 14 B1
Innellan 33 D2
Innerleithen 34 C3
Insch 43 D3
Inveralligan 40 C2
Inverallochy 43 F2
Inveraray 37 E4
Inverarity 39 D3
Inverarnan 37 F4
Inverbervie 39 F1
Invercassley 44 C4
Invercharnan 37 E2
Inverey 38 C1
Invergarry 41 E4
Invergordon 42 A2
Inverinan 37 E4
Inverkeilor 39 E2
Inverkeithing 34 B1
Inverkirkaig 44 A3
Inverlael 41 E1
Invermoriston 41 F4
Inverneil 32 C1
Inverness 42 A3
Inverness Airport 42 A2
Invernoaden 37 E4
Inverurie 43 E4

Ipplepen 5 D2
Ipstones 20 B2
Ipswich 17 E2
Irchester 15 F1
Irlam 25 D4
Ironbridge 20 A3
Irthlingborough 15 F1
Irvine 33 E3
Isbister (Mainland) *Shet.*
　48 B1
Isbister (Whalsay) *Shet.*
　48 C2
Isle of Man Airport 24 A3
Isle of Whithorn 28 C2
Isleham 16 C1
Isleworth 50 C4
Islington 51 E3
Istead Rise 51 H5
Iver 10 A1
Iver 50 B3
Iver Heath 50 B3
Ivinghoe 15 F3
Ivybridge 4 C3
Iwade 17 D3
Ixworth 17 D1

J

Jarrow 31 D1
Jaywick 17 E3
Jedburgh 35 D3
Jemimaville 42 A2
John o' Groats 45 F1
Johnston 12 A2
Johnstone 33 E2
Johnstonebridge 34 B4
Jordans 50 A2

K

Kames 33 D1
Kearsley 25 D4
Kedington 16 C2
Keelby 27 D3
Keele 20 A2
Kegworth 21 D3
Keighley 25 F2
Keillmore 32 C1
Keiss 45 F1
Keith 43 D2
Kellas *Angus* 39 D3
Kellas *Moray* 42 C2
Kelso 35 D3
Kelty 38 C4
Kelvedon 17 D3
Kelvedon Hatch 16 B4
Kelvedon Hatch 51 G2
Kemnay 43 E4
Kempsey 14 B2
Kempston 15 F2
Kendal 30 A4
Kenilworth 14 C1
Kenilworth 53 E4
Kenmore 38 B2
Kennacraig 32 C2
Kennethmont 43 D3
Kennington 15 D3
Kennoway 39 D4
Kensaleyre 40 B2
Kensington & Chelsea
　50 D4
Kensworth 15 F3
Kentallen 37 E2
Kenton *Devon* 5 D2
Keresley 53 F3
Kesgrave 17 E2
Kessingland 23 F4

Keston 51 F5
Keswick 29 F3
Kettering 21 F4
Kettlebrook 53 E1
Kettletoft 49 F2
Kettlewell 25 E1
Ketton 21 F3
Kew 50 C4
Kewstoke 7 F2
Keyingham 27 D3
Keymer 10 B4
Keynsham 8 A1
Keyworth 21 E2
Kidbrooke 51 F4
Kiddemore Green 52 A1
Kidderminster 20 B4
Kidderminster 52 A4
Kidlington 15 D3
Kidsgrove 20 B2
Kidwelly (Cydwelli) 6 B1
Kielder 35 D4
Kilberry 32 C2
Kilbirnie 33 E2
Kilburn *Derbys.* 21 D2
Kilcadzow 34 A2
Kilchattan 36 B4
Kilchenzie 32 C3
Kilchiaran 32 A2
Kilchoan 36 C2
Kilchoman 32 A2
Kilchrenan 37 E3
Kilconquhar 39 E4
Kilcreggan 33 E1
Kildonan Lodge 45 D3
Kildrummy 43 D4
Kilfinan 33 D1
Kilgetty 6 A1
Kilham *E.Riding* 27 D1
Kilham *Nhumb.* 35 E3
Kilkhampton 6 A4
Killamarsh 26 A4
Killay 6 C1
Killean 32 C2
Killearn 33 F1
Killichonan 38 A2
Killiecrankie 38 B2
Killin 38 A3
Killinghall 26 A1
Killingworth 31 D1
Killundine 36 C2
Kilmacolm 33 E1
Kilmalieu 37 D2
Kilmaluag 40 B2
Kilmarnock 33 F3
Kilmartin 37 D4
Kilmaurs 33 E3
Kilmelford 37 D4
Kilmington 5 F1
Kilmory *Arg. & B.* 32 C1
Kilmory (Rum) *High.*
　40 A4
Kilninian 36 B2
Kilninver 37 D3
Kiloran 36 B4
Kilrenny 39 E4
Kilsyth 33 F1
Kilwinning 33 E2
Kimberley *Norf.* 23 D4
Kimberley *Notts.* 21 D2
Kimbolton 16 A1
Kimpton 16 A3
Kinbrace 45 D3
Kincardine 34 A4
Kincardine O'Neil 43 D4
Kincraig 42 A4
Kineton Green 53 D3

Kingarth 33 D2
Kinghorn 34 B1
Kinglassie 39 D4
King's Heath 52 C3
King's Hill 52 B2
Kings Langley 15 F3
Kings Langley 50 B1
King's Lynn 22 C3
King's Norton *W.Mid.*
　52 C4
King's Sutton 15 D2
Kings Worthy 9 E2
Kingsbarns 39 E4
Kingsbridge 4 C3
Kingsbury *Gt.Lon.* **50 C3**
Kingsbury *Warks.* 20 C4
Kingsbury *Warks.* **53 E2**
Kingsbury Episcopi 7 F4
Kingsclere 9 E1
Kingsdown 11 F2
Kingsford *Worcs.* **52 A3**
Kingshouse 38 A3
Kingskerswell 5 D2
Kingsley *Ches.* 19 F1
Kingsley *Staffs.* 20 B2
Kingsnorth 11 E3
Kingstanding 52 C2
Kingsteignton 5 D2
Kingsthorne 13 F4
Kingston 42 C2
Kingston Bagpuize 15 D3
Kingston Seymour 7 F2
Kingston upon Hull
　27 D3
Kingston upon Thames
　50 C4
Kingstone 13 F4
Kingswear 5 D3
Kingswinford 52 A3
Kingswood *S.Glos.*
　14 A4
Kingswood *Surr.* 10 B2
Kingswood *Warks.*
　53 D4
Kington 13 E3
Kingussie 42 A4
Kinloch 40 B4
Kinloch Hourn 41 D4
Kinloch Rannoch 38 A2
Kinlochard 38 A4
Kinlochbervie 44 B2
Kinlocheil 37 E1
Kinlochewe 41 D2
Kinlochleven 37 E2
Kinloss 42 B2
Kinmel Bay 19 D1
Kinross 38 C4
Kintbury 9 D1
Kintore 43 E4
Kintour 32 B2
Kintra 32 A2
Kinver 52 A3
Kippax 26 A3
Kippen 38 A4
Kirby Corner 53 E4
Kirby Muxloe 21 D3
Kirk Michael 24 A2
Kirk Sandall 26 B3
Kirk Yetholm 35 E3
Kirkbean 29 D2
Kirkbride 29 E2
Kirkburton 25 F3
Kirkby *Mersey.* 24 C4
Kirkby in Ashfield 21 D1
Kirkby Lonsdale 25 D1
Kirkby Malzeard 25 F1

Kirkby Stephen 30 B4
Kirkbymoorside 31 E4
Kirkcaldy 34 B1
Kirkcolm 28 A1
Kirkconnel 34 A4
Kirkcowan 28 B2
Kirkcudbright 28 C2
Kirkham 24 C2
Kirkinner 28 B2
Kirkintilloch 33 F1
Kirkliston 34 B1
Kirkmichael *P. & K.* 38 C2
Kirkmichael *S.Ayr.* 33 E4
Kirkmuirhill 34 A2
Kirknewton *Nhumb.*
　35 E3
Kirknewton *W.Loth.*
　34 B2
Kirkoswald *Cumb.* 30 A2
Kirkoswald *S.Ayr.* 33 E4
Kirkpatrick Durham 29 D1
Kirkpatrick-Fleming 29 F1
Kirkton 37 D4
Kirkton of Culsalmond
　43 D3
Kirkton of Durris 39 F1
Kirkton of Glenisla 39 D2
Kirkton of Kingoldrum
　39 D2
Kirkton of Menmuir
　39 E2
Kirkton of Skene 43 E4
Kirktown of Auchterless
　43 E3
Kirktown of Deskford
　43 D2
Kirkwall 49 E3
Kirriemuir 39 D2
Kirtlington 15 D3
Kirton *Lincs.* 22 A2
Kirton *Suff.* 17 E2
Kirton in Lindsey 26 C4
Knaresborough 26 A2
Knayton 31 D4
Knebworth 16 A3
Knighton 13 E2
Knock 36 C3
Knockandhu 42 C4
Knottingley 26 A3
Knotty Green 50 A2
Knowle *W.Mid.* 20 C4
Knowle *W.Mid.* **53 D4**
Knucklas 13 E2
Knutsford 20 A1
Kyle of Lochalsh 40 C3
Kyleakin 40 C3
Kylerhea 40 C4
Kylestrome 44 B2

L

Laceby 27 D4
Lacock 8 B1
Ladybank 39 D4
Ladykirk 35 E2
Ladysford 43 E2
Lagg 33 D3
Laggan (Invergarry)
　High. 37 F1
Laggan (Newtonmore)
　High. 38 A1
Lagganulva 36 C3
Laide 41 D1
Laindon 51 H3
Lairg 44 C4
Lakenheath 16 C1
Laleham 50 B5

Laleston 7 D2
Lamberhurst 11 D3
Lambeth 50 D4
Lambourn 15 D4
Lambourne End 51 F2
Lamlash 33 D3
Lampeter 12 C3
Lamport 15 E1
Lanark 34 A2
Lancaster 24 C1
Lanchester 30 C2
Landore 6 C1
Landywood 52 B1
Lane End *Bucks.* 15 E4
Lane End *Kent* 51 G4
Lane Green 52 A1
Langdon Hills 51 H3
Langford 16 A2
Langham 21 F3
Langholm 29 F1
Langley *Slo.* 50 B4
Langley *Warks.* 53 D5
Langold 26 B4
Langport 7 F4
Langtoft 26 C1
Langwathby 30 A3
Lanivet 4 A2
Lapworth 14 C1
Lapworth 53 D4
Larbert 34 A1
Largoward 39 D4
Largs 33 E2
Larkhall 34 A2
Larkhill 8 C1
Larling 23 D4
Latchingdon 17 D4
Latheron 45 E2
Latheronwheel 45 E3
Latimer 50 B2
Lauder 34 C2
Laugharne 6 B1
Launceston 4 B1
Laurencekirk 39 E2
Lavenham 17 D2
Law 34 A2
Lawers 38 A3
Lawford 17 D3
Laxey 24 B2
Laxford Bridge 44 B2
Laxo 48 B2
Layer de la Haye 17 D3
Lazonby 30 A2
Lea Marston 53 E2
Leadburn 34 B2
Leadenham 21 F2
Leadgate 30 C2
Leadhills 34 A3
Leasingham 21 F2
Leatherhead 10 A2
Leavening 26 C1
Leaves Green 51 F5
Lechlade 14 C3
Leckhampton 14 B3
Leckmelm 41 E1
Ledaig 37 D3
Ledbury 14 A2
Ledmore 44 B3
Lee *Lancs.* 25 D2
Lee Moor 4 C2
Lee-on-the-Solent 9 E3
Leeds *W.Yorks.* 26 A2
Leeds Bradford
  International Airport
  25 F2
Leedstown 3 E3
Leek 20 B1

Leek Wootton 53 E5
Leeming 31 D4
Leicester 21 E3
Leigh *Gt.Man.* 25 D4
Leighton Buzzard 15 F2
Leiston 17 F1
Leith 34 B1
Lenham 11 D2
Lennoxtown 33 F1
Leominster 13 F3
Lerwick 48 B3
Lesbury 35 F4
Leslie 39 D4
Lesmahagow 34 A3
Leswalt 28 A1
Letchmore Heath 50 C2
Letchworth 16 A2
Letheringsett 23 D2
Letterston 12 B1
Leuchars 39 D3
Leumrabhagh 47 E3
Leven *E.Riding* 27 D2
Leven *Fife* 39 D4
Levenwick 48 B4
Leverstock Green 50 B1
Lewes 10 B4
Lewisham 51 E4
Leyburn 30 C4
Leyland 25 D3
Leysdown-on-Sea 11 E1
Leyton 51 E3
Lhanbryde 42 C2
Libberton 34 A2
Lichfield 20 C3
Lichfield 53 D1
Lickey 52 B4
Lickey End 52 B4
Lightwater 9 F1
Lightwater 50 A5
Lilleshall 20 A3
Lilliesleaf 34 C3
Limekilns 34 B1
Lincoln 21 F1
Lincomb 52 A5
Lindfield 10 B3
Lindores 39 D4
Linford *Thur.* 11 D1
Linford *Thur.* 51 H4
Lingfield 10 B2
Linksness 49 D3
Linlithgow 34 A1
Linsidemore 41 F1
Linton 16 B2
Liphook 9 F2
Liskeard 4 B2
Liss 9 F2
Liswerry 7 F2
Litherland 24 C4
Little Aston 52 C2
**Little Berkhamsted
  50 D1**
Little Burstead 51 H2
Little Chalfont 50 A2
Little Clacton 17 E3
Little Common 11 D4
Little Downham 16 B1
Little Eaton 21 D2
Little End 51 G1
Little Hay 53 D1
Little Heath 53 F3
Little Laver 51 G1
Little Missenden 15 F3
Little Missenden 50 A2
Little Oakley 17 E3
Little Parndon 51 F1
Little Paxton 16 A1
Little Plumstead 23 E3

Little Thurrock 51 H4
Little Warley 51 H2
Little Wyrley 52 C1
Littleborough 25 E3
Littlebourne 11 F2
Littledean 14 A3
Littlehampton 10 A4
Littlemill *E.Ayr.* 33 F4
Littlemill *High.* 42 B2
Littlemore 15 D3
Littleport 22 B4
Littlestone-on-Sea 11 E3
Littleton *Surr.* 50 B5
Liverpool 19 E1
Liversedge 25 F3
Livingston 34 B1
Lizard 3 E4
Llanaelhaearn 18 B2
Llanarth 12 B3
Llanarthney 12 B4
Llanbadarn Fawr 12 C2
Llanbadrig 18 A1
Llanbedr 18 B3
Llanbedrog 18 A3
Llanberis 18 B2
Llanbister 13 E2
Llanblethian 7 D2
Llanddarog 12 B4
Llanddeiniolen 18 B2
Llandderfel 19 D3
Llanddowror 6 A1
Llandeilo 12 C4
Llandinam 13 D2
Llandissilio 12 A4
Llandovery 12 C4
Llandrillo 19 D3
Llandrindod Wells 13 E3
Llandudno 18 C1
Llandwrog 18 B2
Llandybie 12 C4
Llandysul 12 B4
Llanegwad 12 B4
Llanelli 6 B1
Llanelltyd 18 C3
Llanelly 13 E4
Llanelwy (St. Asaph)
  19 D1
Llanerch-y-medd 18 B1
Llanfaelog 18 A1
Llanfair Caereinion 13 E1
Llanfair Talhaiarn 19 D1
Llanfairfechan 18 C1
Llanfairpwllgwyngyll
  18 B1
Llanfihangel ar-arth
  12 B4
Llanfyllin 19 D3
Llanfynydd 19 E2
Llangadfan 13 D1
Llangadog 12 C4
Llangefni 18 B1
Llangeler 12 B4
Llangelynin 12 C1
Llangendeirne 6 B1
Llangernyw 18 C2
Llangoed 18 B1
Llangollen 19 E3
Llangranog 12 B3
Llangunnor 12 B4
Llangurig 13 D2
Llangwm 12 B2
Llangynidr 13 E4
Llanharan 7 D2
Llanhilleth 7 E1
Llanidloes 13 D2
Llanilar 12 C2
Llanishen *Cardiff* 7 E2

Llanllwchaiarn 13 E2
Llanllyfni 18 B2
Llannon 6 B1
Llanon 12 B2
Llanrhaeadr-ym
  Mochnant 19 D3
Llanrhidian 6 B1
Llanrhystud 12 B2
Llanrug 18 B2
Llanrumney 7 E2
Llanrwst 18 C2
Llansamlet 6 C1
Llansannan 19 D2
Llansantffraid Glan
  Conwy 18 C1
Llansawel 12 C4
Llansteffan 6 B1
Llanthony 13 E4
Llantilio Pertholey 13 F4
Llantrisant *Mon.* 7 F1
Llantrisant *R.C.T.* 7 D2
Llantwit Major 7 D2
Llanuwchllyn 18 C3
Llanwddyn 19 D3
Llanwnda 18 B2
Llanwnog 13 D1
Llanwrda 12 C4
Llanwrtyd Wells 13 D3
Llanybydder 12 B3
Llanynghenedl 18 A1
Llanystumdwy 18 B3
Lledrod 12 C2
Loanhead 34 B2
Loans 33 D3
Loch Baghasdail
  (Lochboisdale) 46 B3
Loch na Madadh
  (Lochmaddy) 46 B1
Loch Sgioport 46 B2
Lochailort 37 D1
Lochaline 36 C3
Lochans 28 A2
Locharbriggs 29 E1
Lochawe 37 E3
Lochboisdale (Loch
  Baghasdail) 46 B3
Lochcarron 41 D3
Lochdon 37 D3
Lochearnhead 38 A3
Lochend 41 F3
Lochgelly 34 B1
Lochgilphead 32 C1
Lochgoilhead 37 F4
Lochinver 44 A3
Lochmaben 29 E1
Lochmaddy (Loch na
  Madadh) 46 B1
Lochranza 33 D2
Lochwinnoch 33 E2
Lockerbie 29 E1
Locking 7 F3
Locks Heath 9 E3
Locksbottom 51 F5
Lockton 31 F4
Loddiswell 4 C3
Loddon 23 E4
Lofthouse *W.Yorks.*
  26 A3
Loftus 31 E3
Logan 33 F3
Loggerheads 20 A2
London 10 B1
London City Airport 51 F3
London Colney 16 A4
London Colney 50 C1
London Heathrow Airport
  10 A1

**London Heathrow
  Airport 50 B4**
London Luton Airport
  16 A3
Long Ashton 7 F2
Long Bennington 21 F2
Long Buckby 15 E1
Long Compton 14 C2
Long Crendon 15 E3
Long Ditton 50 C5
Long Eaton 21 D2
Long Hanborough 15 D3
Long Itchington 15 D1
Long Lawford 21 D4
Long Melford 17 D2
Long Preston 25 E1
Long Stratton 23 E4
Long Sutton *Lincs.*
  22 B3
Long Sutton *Som.* 7 F4
Longbenton 31 D1
**Longbridge *Warks.*
  53 E5**
**Longbridge *W.Mid.*
  52 C4**
Longbridge Deverill 8 B2
Longcross *Surr.* 50 A5
Longdon 20 C3
Longfield 51 H5
Longfield Hill 51 H5
Longford *Gt.Lon.* 50 B4
Longford *W.Mid.* 53 F3
Longforgan 39 D3
Longframlington 35 F4
Longhope *Glos.* 14 A3
Longhope *Ork.* 49 D4
Longhorsley 35 F4
Longhoughton 35 F3
Longmanhill 43 E2
Longmorn 42 C2
Longniddry 34 C1
Longridge 25 D2
Longside 43 F3
Longton *Lancs.* 24 C3
Longtown 29 F1
Looe 4 B3
Loose 11 D2
Lopcombe Corner 9 D2
Loscoe 21 D2
Lossiemouth 42 C2
Lostwithiel 4 A2
Loth 49 F2
Lothmore 45 E3
Loughborough 21 D3
Loughor 6 C1
Loughton *Essex* 16 B4
Loughton *Essex* 51 F2
Louth 22 A1
Loves Green 51 H1
Low Habberley 52 A4
Low Street 23 E3
Lowdham 21 E2
Lower Beeding 10 B3
Lower Cam 14 A3
Lower Diabaig 40 C2
**Lower Green *Staffs.*
  52 B1**
Lower Killeyan 32 A2
Lower Nazeing 51 E1
Lower Penn 52 A2
Lowestoft 23 F4
Loweswater 29 E3
Lowick 35 E3
Lowsonford 53 D5
Ludag 46 A3
Luddesdown 51 H5
Ludgershall 9 D1

Ludgvan 3 D3
Ludlow 13 F2
Luib 40 B3
Lumphanan 43 D4
Luncarty 38 C3
Lundin Links 39 D4
Luss 33 E1
Lusta 40 A2
Luton 16 A3
Lutterworth 21 D4
Luxulyan 4 A3
Lybster 45 F2
Lydd 11 E3
Lydd Airport 11 E3
Lydford 4 C1
Lydiate 24 C4
Lydney 14 A3
Lye 52 B3
Lye Green 50 A1
Lyme Regis 5 F1
Lyminge 11 E3
Lymington 9 D3
Lymm 25 D4
Lympne 11 E3
Lympstone 5 D2
Lyndhurst 9 D3
Lyne Surr. 50 B5
Lyne of Skene 43 E4
Lyneham 14 B4
Lynemore 42 B3
Lynemouth 35 F4
Lyness 49 D4
Lynmouth 6 C3
Lynton 6 C3
Lytchett Matravers 8 B3
Lytchett Minster 8 C3
Lytham St. Anne's 24 C3

M

Mablethorpe 22 B1
Macclesfield 20 B1
Macduff 43 E2
Macharioch 32 C4
Machen 7 E1
Machrihanish 32 B3
Machynlleth 12 C1
Macmerry 34 C1
Madeley Staffs. 20 A2
Madley 13 F4
Madron 3 D3
Maenclochog 12 A4
Maentwrog 18 C3
Maerdy 7 D1
Maesteg 7 D1
Magdalen Laver 51 G1
Maghull 24 C4
Maiden Bradley 8 B2
Maiden Newton 8 A3
Maidenhead 15 F4
Maidens 33 E4
Maidstone 11 D2
Malden 50 D5
Malden Rushett 50 C5
Maldon 17 D4
Mallaig 36 C1
Mallwyd 13 D1
Malmesbury 14 B4
Malpas 7 E1
Malpas Ches. 19 F2
Maltby S.Yorks. 26 B4
Maltby le Marsh 22 B1
Malton 26 C1
Malvern Link 14 A2
Manby 22 B1
Mancetter 20 C4
Mancetter 53 F2

Manchester 25 E4
Manchester Airport
  25 E4
Manea 22 B4
Mangotsfield 14 A4
Manningtree 17 E3
Manorbier 6 A1
Mansfield 21 D1
Mansfield Woodhouse
  21 D1
Manston 8 B3
Maple Cross 50 B2
**Mappleborough Green
  52 C5**
Marazion 3 E3
March 22 B4
Marchwiel 19 E2
Marden Kent 11 D2
Mareham le Fen 22 A2
Maresfield 10 C3
Margam 6 C2
Margaretting 51 H1
Margate 11 F1
Marham 22 C3
Mark 7 F3
Market Bosworth 21 D3
Market Deeping 22 A3
Market Drayton 20 A2
Market Harborough
  21 E4
Market Lavington 8 C1
Market Rasen 27 D4
Market Weighton 26 C2
Markfield 21 D3
Markinch 39 D4
Marks Gate 51 F3
Marks Tey 17 D3
Markyate 15 F3
Marlborough 8 C1
Marldon 5 D2
Marlow 15 F4
Marnhull 8 B2
Marple 25 E4
Marsden W.Yorks. 25 F3
Marshfield S.Glos.
  14 A4
Marske-by-the-Sea 31 E3
Marston Oxon. 15 D3
Marston Warks. 53 E2
Marston Green 53 D3
Marston Magna 8 A2
Marston Moretaine 15 F2
Martham 23 F3
Martlesham 17 E2
Martley 14 A1
Martock 7 F4
Marybank 41 F2
Marykirk 39 E2
**Marylebone Gt.Lon.
  50 D3**
Marypark 42 C3
Maryport 29 E2
Marywell 39 E1
Masham 25 F1
Matlock 20 C1
Matlock Bath 20 C1
Mauchline 33 F3
Maud 43 F3
Maughold 24 B2
Maw Green 52 C2
Maxstoke 53 E2
Maybole 33 E4
Mayfield 20 C2
Mealsgate 29 E2
Meare 7 F3
Measham 21 D3
Medstead 9 E2

Meer End 53 E4
Meidrim 12 A4
Meigle 39 D3
Meikle Kilmory 33 D2
Meikleour 38 C3
Melbourn 16 B2
Melbourne 21 D3
Melksham 8 B1
Melmerby 30 A2
Melrose 34 C3
Melsonby 30 C4
Meltham 25 F3
Melton 17 E2
Melton Mowbray 21 E3
Melvaig 40 C1
Melvich 45 D1
Memsie 43 F2
Menai Bridge 18 B1
Menston 25 F2
Menstrie 38 B4
Meopham 51 H5
Meopham Green 51 H5
Mere Wilts. 8 B2
Mere Green 53 D2
Meriden 20 C4
Meriden 53 E3
Merry Hill 50 C2
Merthyr Tydfil 7 D1
Merton Gt.Lon. 50 D5
Messingham 26 C4
Metfield 17 E1
Metheringham 21 F1
Methlick 43 E3
Methven 38 C3
Methwold 22 C4
Mevagissey 4 A3
Mexborough 26 A4
Mey 45 F1
Miabhig 47 D2
Mickleton Dur. 30 B3
Mickleton Glos. 14 C2
Mid Ardlaw 43 F2
Mid Yell 48 C1
Midbea 49 E2
Middle Barton 15 D2
Middle Rasen 27 D4
Middleham 30 C4
Middlemarsh 8 A3
Middlesbrough 31 D3
Middlesmoor 25 F1
Middleton Gt.Man.
  25 E4
Middleton Norf. 22 C3
Middleton Warks. 53 D2
Middleton Cheney 15 D2
Middleton Stoney 15 D3
Middleton-in-Teesdale
  30 B3
Middleton-on-Sea 10 A4
Middleton-on-the-Wolds
  26 C2
Middlewich 20 A1
Midhurst 9 F2
Midlem 34 C3
Midsomer Norton 8 A1
Milborne Port 8 A2
Milborne St. Andrew
  8 B3
Mildenhall 16 C1
Mile End 17 D3
Milfield 35 E3
Milford Surr. 9 F2
Milford Haven 12 A2
Milford on Sea 9 D4
Mill Green Essex 51 H1
Mill Hill 50 D2
Millbrook Cornw. 4 B3

Millhouse 33 D1
Millom 24 B1
Millport 33 D2
Milltown of Rothiemay
  43 D3
Milnathort 38 C4
Milngavie 33 F1
Milnrow 25 E3
Milnthorpe 24 C1
Milovaig 40 A2
Milton High. 41 F3
Milton P. & K. 38 B3
Milton Keynes 15 F2
Milton of Campsie 33 F1
Milverton 7 E4
Minard 37 E4
Minchinhampton 14 B3
Minehead 7 D3
Minera 19 E2
Minnigaff 28 B1
Minster (Sheppey) Kent
  11 E1
Minster (Thanet) Kent
  11 F2
Minsterley 13 F1
Mintlaw 43 F3
Minworth 53 D2
Mirfield 25 F3
Misterton 26 B4
Mitcham 50 D5
Mitcheldean 14 A3
Mobberley 20 A1
Modbury 4 C3
Moelfre 18 B1
Moffat 34 B4
Mold 19 E2
Molescroft 27 D2
Moniaive 34 A4
Monifieth 39 E3
Monimail 39 D4
Monken Hadley 50 D2
Monkokehampton 4 C1
Monks Eleigh 17 D2
Monmore Green 52 B2
Monmouth (Trefynwy)
  7 F1
Monreith 28 B2
Montgomery
  (Trefaldwyn)
  13 E1
Montrose 39 E2
Moorends 26 B3
Morar 36 C1
Morden Gt.Lon. 50 D5
Morebattle 35 D3
Morecambe 24 C1
Morenish 38 A3
Moresby 29 E3
Moreton Essex 51 G1
Moreton Mersey. 19 E1
Moreton-in-Marsh
  14 C2
Moretonhampstead
  5 D1
Morfa Nefyn 18 A3
Morley W.Yorks. 26 A3
Morpeth 30 C1
Morriston 6 C1
Mortehoe 6 B3
Mortimer's Cross 13 F3
Mortlake 50 D4
Morton (Bourne) Lincs.
  22 A3
Morton (Gainsborough)
  Lincs. 26 C4
Morton Bagot 53 D5
Morville 20 A4

Mosborough 26 A4
Moscow 33 F3
Moseley W.Mid. 52 C3
Mossat 43 D4
Mossblown 33 E3
Mossley 25 E4
Mosstodloch 42 C2
Motherwell 34 A2
Mottingham 51 F4
Moulsecoomb 10 B4
Moulton Lincs. 22 A3
Moulton Suff. 16 C1
Mountain Ash 7 E1
Mountbenger 34 C3
Mountnessing 51 H2
Mountsorrel 21 E3
Moxley 52 B2
Moy 42 A3
Much Wenlock 20 A4
Muchalls 39 F1
Muir of Fowlis 43 D4
Muir of Ord 41 F2
Muirdrum 39 E3
Muirhead Angus 39 D3
Muirkirk 33 F3
Mulbarton 23 E4
Mulben 42 C2
Mullion 3 E4
Mundesley 23 E2
Mundford 22 C4
Munlochy 42 A2
Murton 31 D2
Musbury 5 F1
Musselburgh 34 C1
Mustow Green 52 A4
Muthill 38 B4
Mybster 45 E2
Mytholmroyd 25 E3

N

Nailsea 7 F2
Nailsworth 14 B3
Nairn 42 A2
Nantwich 20 A2
Nantyglo 7 F1
Narberth 6 A1
Narborough Leics.
  21 D4
Narborough Norf. 22 C3
Nateby 30 B4
Navestock 51 G2
Navestock Side 51 G2
Nazeing 16 B4
Nazeing 51 F1
Neal's Green 53 F3
Near Sawrey 29 F4
Neath 6 C1
Necton 23 D4
Needham Market 17 D2
Needingworth 16 B1
Nefyn 18 A3
Neilston 33 F2
Nelson 25 E2
Nenthead 30 B2
Neston 19 E1
Nether Langwith 21 D1
Nether Stowey 7 E3
Nether Whitacre 53 E2
Netherley 39 F1
Netherton Nhumb. 35 E4
Netherton W.Mid. 52 B3
Netherton W.Yorks. 25 F3
Nethy Bridge 42 B4
Nettlebed 15 E4
Nettleham 21 F1
New Abbey 29 D1

New Aberdour 43 E2
New Addington 10 B2
New Addington 51 E5
New Alresford 9 E2
New Arley 53 E2
New Ash Green 10 C2
New Ash Green 51 H5
New Barn 51 H5
New Barnet 50 D2
New Byth 43 E2
New Cumnock 33 F4
New Deer 43 E3
New Eltham 51 F4
New Galloway 28 C1
New Haw 50 B5
**New Invention W.Mid.
52 B1**
New Leeds 43 F2
New Luce 28 A1
New Malden 50 D5
New Mills 25 E4
New Milton 9 D3
New Mistley 17 E3
New Pitsligo 43 E2
New Quay 12 B3
New Radnor 13 E3
New Romney 11 E3
New Rossington 26 B4
New Scone 38 C3
New Tredegar 7 E1
Newark-on-Trent 21 E1
Newbiggin-by-the-Sea
31 D1
Newbigging 34 A2
Newbold Verdon 21 D3
Newbridge Caerp. 7 E1
Newburgh Aber. 43 F3
Newburgh Fife 39 D4
Newburn 30 C1
Newbury 9 E1
Newby Bridge 29 F4
Newcastle Shrop. 13 E2
Newcastle Emlyn 12 B4
Newcastle International
Airport 30 C1
Newcastle upon Tyne
30 C1
Newcastle-under-Lyme
20 B2
Newcastleton 29 F1
Newent 14 A2
Newgate Street 51 E1
Newham Gt.Lon. 51 E3
Newhaven 10 C4
Newick 10 B3
Newington 11 D2
Newlyn 3 D3
Newmachar 43 E4
Newmains 34 A2
Newmarket Suff. 16 C1
Newmarket W.Isles 47 F2
Newmill 43 D2
Newmilns 33 F3
Newnham 14 A3
Newport Essex 16 B2
Newport High. 45 E3
Newport I.o.W. 9 E4
Newport Newport 7 F2
Newport Pembs. 12 A4
Newport Tel. & W. 20 A3
Newport Pagnell 15 F2
Newport-on-Tay 39 D3
Newquay 3 F2
Newton Arg. & B. 37 E4
Newton (Bowland)
Lancs. 25 D2

Newton Abbot 5 D2
Newton Aycliffe 31 D3
**Newton Burgoland
53 F1**
Newton Ferrers 4 C3
Newton Mearns 33 F2
Newton Poppleford 5 E1
Newton Regis 53 E1
Newton St. Cyres 5 D1
Newton Stewart 28 B1
Newton-le-Willows 19 F1
Newtonhill 39 F1
Newtonmore 42 A4
Newtown Bucks. 50 A1
Newtown Here. 14 A2
Newtown (Y Drenewydd)
Powys 13 E2
Newtown St. Boswells
35 D3
Newtyle 39 D3
Neyland 12 B2
Nine Ashes 51 G1
Ninemile Bar or
Crocketford 29 D1
Ninfield 11 D4
Nisbet 35 D3
**No Man's Heath Warks.
53 E1**
Noak Hill 51 G2
Norbiton 50 C5
Norchard 52 A5
Norham 35 E2
Normanton W.Yorks.
26 A3
North Baddesley 9 D2
North Ballachulish 37 E2
North Berwick 34 C1
North Cave 26 C2
North Cheriton 8 A2
North Cowton 31 D4
North Cray 51 F4
North Duffield 26 B2
North Elmham 23 D3
North Ferriby 26 C3
North Grimston 26 C1
North Hykeham 21 F1
North Kessock 42 A3
North Leigh 15 D3
North Middleton 34 C2
North Molton 6 C4
North Ockendon 51 G3
North Queensferry 34 B1
North Shields 31 D1
North Somercotes 27 E4
North Stifford 51 H3
North Sunderland 35 F3
North Thoresby 27 E4
North Tidworth 9 D1
North Walsham 23 E3
North Weald Bassett
16 B4
North Weald Bassett 51 F1
North Wingfield D1
Northallerton 31 D4
Northam Devon 6 B4
Northampton 15 E1
Northaw 50 D1
Northchurch 50 A1
Northfield W.Mid. 52 C4
Northfleet 10 C1
Northfleet 51 H4
Northill 16 A2
Northleach 14 C3
Northolt 50 C3
Northwich 20 A1
Northwood Gt.Lon. 50 B2
Northwood I.o.W. 9 E3

Norton N.Yorks. 26 C1
Norton Suff. 17 D1
Norton W.Mid. 52 A3
Norton Canes 20 B3
Norton Canes 52 C1
Norton Fitzwarren 7 E4
Norton Heath 51 H1
Norton Lindsey 53 E5
Norton Mandeville 51 G1
**Norton-Juxta-Twycross
53 F1**
Norwich 23 E4
Norwich Airport 23 E3
Norwick 48 C1
Norwood Green 50 C4
Nottingham 21 D2
Nuneaton 21 D4
Nuneaton 53 F2
Nurton 52 A2
Nuthurst Warks. 53 D4

O

Oadby 21 E4
Oakdale 7 E1
Oaken 52 A1
Oakengates 20 A3
Oakham 21 F3
Oakley Bucks. 15 E3
Oakley Fife 34 A1
Oakley Hants. 9 E1
Oakley Green 50 A4
Oban 37 D3
Ochiltree 33 F3
Ockbrook 21 D2
Ockle 36 C2
Oddsta 48 C1
Odiham 9 F1
Odstone 53 F1
Offchurch 53 F5
Ogmore 7 D2
Ogmore Vale 7 D1
Okehampton 4 C1
Old Arley 53 E2
Old Colwyn 18 C1
Old Dailly 33 E4
Old Felixstowe 17 E2
Old Hill 52 B3
Old Leake 22 B2
Old Town 25 D1
Old Windsor 50 A4
Oldberrow 53 D5
Oldbury Warks. 53 F2
Oldbury W.Mid. 20 B4
Oldbury W.Mid. 52 B2
Oldfield Worcs. 52 A5
Oldham 25 E4
Oldland 8 A1
Oldmeldrum 43 E3
Olgrinmore 45 E2
Ollaberry 48 B2
Ollerton Notts. 21 E1
Olney 15 F1
Olveston 14 A4
Ombersley 14 B1
Ombersley 52 A5
Onchan 24 B3
Onich 37 E2
Orford Suff. 17 F2
Ormesby St. Margaret
23 F3
Ormiston 34 C1
Ormskirk 24 C3
Orpington 10 C2

Orpington 51 F5
Orrell 25 D3
Orsett 51 H3
Orton 30 A4
Orton Longueville 22 A4
Orton-on-the-Hill 53 F1
Oskaig 40 B3
Ossett 26 A3
Osterley 50 C4
Oswaldkirk 26 B1
Oswaldtwistle 25 D3
Oswestry 19 E3
Otford 10 C2
Otley Suff. 17 E2
Otley W.Yorks. 25 F2
Otter Ferry 33 D1
Otterburn 35 E4
Ottershaw 50 B5
Otterswick 48 C2
Ottery St. Mary 5 E1
Oughtibridge 26 A4
Oulton Suff. 23 F4
Oundle 21 F4
Outwell 22 B4
Over Wallop 9 D2
Over Whitacre 53 E2
Overbister 49 F2
Overseal 20 C3
Overton Hants. 9 E1
Overton Wrex. 19 E3
Overtown 34 A2
Oxenhope 25 F2
Oxford 15 D3
Oxley 52 B1
Oxnam 35 D3
Oxshott 10 A2
Oxshott 50 C5
Oxted 10 B2
Oxton Sc.Bord. 34 C2
Oykel Bridge 41 F1

P

Padbury 15 E2
Paddington 50 D3
Paddock Wood 11 D2
Padiham 25 E2
Padstow 3 F2
Paignton 5 D2
Painswick 14 B3
Paisley 33 F2
Palnackie 29 D2
Pandy 13 F4
Pangbourne 15 E4
Pant-y-dwr 13 D2
Papworth Everard 16 A1
Par 4 A3
Parbold 24 C3
Park Street 50 C1
Parkgate 29 E1
Partington 25 D4
Partney 22 B1
Parton 29 D3
Passingford Bridge 51 F2
Patchway 14 A4
Pateley Bridge 25 F1
Path of Condie 38 C4
Patna 33 E4
Patrick 24 A2
Patrington 27 E3
Patterdale 29 F3
Pattingham 52 A2
Paulton 8 A1
Paxton 35 E2
Peacehaven 10 B4
Peasedown St. John 8 B1
Pedmore 52 B3

Peebles 34 B2
Peel 24 A2
Pegswood 30 C1
Peinchorran 40 B3
Pelsall 20 B3
Pelsall 52 C1
Pelynt 4 A3
Pembrey 6 B1
Pembridge 13 F3
Pembroke 12 B2
Pembroke Dock 12 B2
Pembury 10 C3
Pen-y-bont-fawr 19 D3
Penally 6 A1
Penarth 7 E2
Pencader 12 B4
Pencaitland 34 C1
Pencoed 7 D2
Pendeen 3 D3
Pendlebury 25 E4
Penge 51 E4
Penicuik 34 B2
Peninver 32 C3
Penistone 25 F4
Penkridge 20 B3
Penley 19 F3
Penn Bucks. 50 A2
Penn W.Mid. 52 A2
Penn Street 50 A2
Pennyghael 36 C3
Penpont 34 A4
Penrhiw-pal 12 B3
Penrhyn Bay 18 C1
Penrhyndeudraeth 18 B3
Penrith 30 A3
Penryn 3 F3
Pensilva 4 B2
Pensnett 52 B3
Pentir 18 B2
Pentraeth 18 B1
Pentre 7 D1
Pentrefoelas 18 C2
Penwortham 25 D3
Penybont 13 E3
Penygraig 7 D1
Penygroes 18 B2
Penywaun 7 D1
Penzance 3 D3
Perivale 50 C3
Perranporth 3 E2
Perry Barr 52 C2
Perry Street 51 H4
Pershore 14 B2
Perth 38 C3
Perton 52 A2
Peterborough 22 A4
Peterculter 43 E4
Peterhead 43 F3
Peterlee 31 D2
Petersfield 9 F2
Petworth 10 A3
Pevensey 10 C4
Pewsey 8 C1
Piccotts End 50 B1
Pickerells 51 G1
Pickering 31 F4
Pickford Green 53 E3
Piddletrenthide 8 B3
Pierowall 49 E2
Pilgrims Hatch 16 B4
Pilgrims Hatch 51 G2
Pilling 24 C2
Pilning 7 F2
Pimperne 8 B3
Pinchbeck 22 A3

Pinhoe 5 D1
Pinley Green 53 E5
Pinner 50 C3
Pinner Green 50 C2
Pinwherry 28 A1
Pirbright 9 F1
Pirnmill 32 C2
Pitagowan 38 B2
Pitlochry 38 B2
Pitmedden 43 E3
Pitscottie 39 D4
Pitt 9 D2
Pittentrail 42 A1
Pittenweem 39 E4
Plean 34 A1
Pleasley 21 D1
Plumstead *Gt.Lon.*
51 F4
Plwmp 12 B3
Plymouth 4 C3
Plymouth City Airport
4 C2
Plympton 4 C3
Plymstock 4 C3
Pocklington 26 C2
Polbeth 34 A2
Polegate 10 C4
Polesworth 20 C3
Polesworth 53 E1
Polloch 37 D2
Polmont 34 A1
Polperro 4 A3
Polwarth 35 D2
Ponders End 51 E2
Pondersbridge 22 A4
Pontardawe 6 C1
Pontarddulais 6 C1
Pontefract 26 A3
Ponteland 30 C1
Pontesbury 13 F1
Pontllanfraith 7 E1
Pontrhydfendigaid 12 C3
Pontrilas 13 F4
Pontyberem 6 B1
Pontycymer 7 D1
Pontypool 7 E1
Pontypridd 7 E1
Pool 25 F2
Poole 8 C4
Poolewe 40 C1
Pooley Bridge 29 F3
Poplar 51 E3
Porlock 7 D3
Port Appin 37 D3
Port Askaig 32 B1
Port Bannatyne 33 D2
Port Driseach 33 D1
Port Ellen 32 A2
Port Erin 24 A3
Port Eynon 6 B2
Port Glasgow 33 E1
Port Henderson 40 C2
Port Logan 28 A2
Port nan Giúran 47 F2
Port nan Long 46 B1
Port Nis 47 F1
Port of Menteith 38 A4
Port St. Mary 24 A3
Port Talbot 6 C1
Port William 28 B2
Portchester 9 E3
Portencross 33 D2
Portesham 8 A4
Porth 7 D1
Porthcawl 7 D2
Porthleven 3 E4
Porthmadog 18 B3

Portishead 7 F2
Portknockie 43 D2
Portlethen 39 F1
Portmahomack 42 B1
Portnacroish 37 D2
Portnahaven 32 A2
Portnalong 40 A3
Portnancon 44 B1
Portpatrick 28 A2
Portreath 3 E3
Portree 40 B3
Portsmouth 9 E3
Portsoy 43 D2
Portway *Worcs.* 52 C4
Potten End 50 B1
Potter Street 51 F1
Potterne 8 C1
Potters Bar 16 A4
Potters Bar 50 D1
Potter's Cross 52 A3
Potters Crouch 50 C1
Potton 16 A2
Poulton-le-Fylde 24 C2
Powburn 35 F3
Powick 14 B1
Powmill 38 C4
Poyle 50 B4
Poynton 25 E4
Pratt's Bottom 51 F5
Prees 19 F3
Preesall 24 C2
Prescot 19 F1
Ratcliffe Culey 53 F2
Prestatyn 19 D1
Prestbury *Ches.* 20 B1
Prestbury *Glos.* 14 B3
Presteigne 13 F3
Preston *Dorset* 8 B4
Preston *E.Riding* 27 D3
Preston *Lancs.* 25 D3
Preston *Sc.Bord.* 35 D2
Preston Bagot 53 D5
Prestonpans 34 C1
Prestwich 25 E4
Prestwick 33 E3
Prestwick International
Airport 33 E3
Prestwood 15 F3
Princes End 52 B2
Princes Risborough
15 E3
Princethorpe 15 D1
Princetown 4 C2
Probus 3 F3
Prudhoe 30 C2
Puddletown 8 B3
Pudsey 25 F2
Pulborough 10 A3
Pumsaint 12 C3
Purfleet 10 C1
Purfleet 51 G4
Puriton 7 F3
Purley 10 B2
Purley 51 E5
Purley on Thames 15 E4
Purton 14 C4
Putney 50 D4
Pwllheli 18 A3
Pyle 7 D2

Q

Quarry Bank 52 B3
Quedgeley 14 A3
Queenborough 11 D1
Queensbury 25 F3
Queensferry 19 E2
Queniborough 21 E3

Quernmore 25 D1
Queslett 52 C2
Quinton *W.Mid.* 52 B3

R

Rackheath 23 E3
Radcliffe *Gt.Man.* 25 E3
Radcliffe on Trent 21 E2
Radford *W.Mid.* 53 F3
Radford Semele 15 D1
Radford Semele 53 F5
Radlett 16 A4
Radlett 50 C1
Radstock 8 A1
Rafford 42 B2
Raglan 7 F1
Rainford 24 C4
Rainham *Gt.Lon.* 51 G3
Rainhill 19 F1
Rainow 20 B1
Rainworth 21 E1
Rait 39 D3
Rampside 24 C1
Ramsbottom 25 E3
Ramsbury 14 C4
Ramsey *Cambs.* 16 A1
Ramsey *I.o.M.* 24 B2
Ramsey St. Mary's 22 A4
Ramsgate 11 F2
Ranskill 26 B4
Rathillet 39 D3
Ratho 34 B1
Rattray 38 C3
Raunds 15 F1
Ravenglass 29 E4
Ravenshead 21 D2
Rawcliffe *E.Riding* 26 B3
Rawcliffe *York* 26 B2
Rawmarsh 26 A4
Rawtenstall 25 E3
Rayleigh 11 D1
Rayne 16 C3
Reading 15 E4
Reay 45 D1
Red Roses 6 A1
Redbourn 16 A3
Redbridge 51 F3
Redcar 31 E3
Redcastle 41 F3
Redcliff Bay 7 F2
Redditch 14 B1
Redditch 52 C5
Redford 39 E3
Redhill *Surr.* 10 B2
Redlynch 8 C2
Rednal *W.Mid.* 52 C4
Redpoint 40 C2
Redruth 3 E3
Reepham 23 E3
Reigate 10 B2
Reiss 45 F2
Renfrew 33 F2
Rennington 35 F3
Repton 20 C3
Rescobie 39 E2
Resolven 7 D1
Reston 35 E2
Retford (East Retford)
21 E1
Reydon 17 F1
Rhayader 13 D2
Rhiconich 44 B2
Rhoose 7 E2
Rhos 6 C1
Rhôs-on-Sea 18 C1

Rhosllanerchrugog 19 E2
Rhossili 6 B2
Rhu 33 E1
Rhuddlan 19 D1
Rhyl 19 D1
Rhymney 7 E1
Rhynie 43 D3
Ribchester 25 D2
Richings Park 50 B4
Richmond 30 C4
Richmond upon Thames
50 C4
Rickarton 39 F1
Rickinghall 17 D1
Rickmansworth 10 A1
Rickmansworth 50 B2
Ridge *Herts.* 50 D1
Ridge Lane 53 E3
Riding Mill 30 C2
Ridley 51 H5
Rigside 34 A3
Ringford 28 C2
Ringmer 10 C4
Ringwood 8 C3
Ripley *Derbys.* 21 D2
Ripley *N.Yorks.* 26 A1
Ripon 26 A1
Ripple 14 B2
Ripponden 25 F3
Risca 7 E1
Rishton 25 D3
Risley 21 D2
Roade 15 E1
Roadside 45 E1
Roadside of Kinneff
39 F1
Roath 7 E2
Roberton *Sc.Bord.* 34 C4
Roberton *S.Lan.* 34 A3
Robin Hood's Bay 31 F4
Rocester 20 C2
Rochdale 25 E3
Roche 4 A2
Rochester *Medway*
11 D2
Rochester *Nhumb.*
35 E4
Rochford 11 D1
Rock 14 A1
Rockcliffe 29 D2
Rockingham 21 F4
Rode Heath 20 A1
Rodney Stoke 7 F3
Roehampton 50 D4
Rogart 45 D3
Rogate 9 F2
Rogerstone 7 E2
Roghadal 47 D4
Romannobridge 34 B2
Romford *Gt.Lon.* 10 C1
Romford *Gt.Lon.* 51 G3
Romney Street 51 G5
Romsey 9 D2
Romsley *Worcs.* 20 B4
Romsley *Worcs.* 52 B3
Ropley 9 E2
Ropsley 21 F2
Rosedale Abbey 31 E4
Rosehearty 43 F2
Rosemarkie 42 A2
Rosewell 34 B2
Roshven 37 D1
Roskhill 40 A3
Roslin 34 B2
Ross-on-Wye 14 A2
Rossett 19 E2
Rossington 26 B4

Rothbury 35 E4
Rotherfield 10 C3
Rotherham 26 A4
Rothes 42 C3
Rothesay 33 D2
Rothiesholm 49 F3
Rothley 21 E3
Rothwell *Northants.*
21 E4
Rothwell *W.Yorks.*
26 A3
Rottingdean 10 B4
Roughley 53 D2
Roughton 23 E2
Roundway 8 C1
Row Town 50 B5
Rowde 8 C1
Rowington 53 E5
Rowington Green 53 E4
Rowlands Gill 30 C2
Rowley Regis 52 B3
Rowney Green 52 C4
Roxton 16 A2
Roxwell 51 H1
Royal Leamington Spa
14 C1
Royal Leamington Spa
53 F5
Royal Tunbridge Wells
10 C3
Roybridge 37 F1
Roydon 17 D1
Roydon Hamlet 51 F1
Royston *Herts.* 16 B2
Royston *S.Yorks.*
26 A3
Royton 25 E3
Ruabon 19 E3
Ruardean 14 A3
Rubery 52 B4
Ruddington 21 E2
Rudgwick 10 A3
Rudston 27 D1
Rufford 24 C3
Rugby 15 D1
Rugeley 20 B3
Ruislip 50 B3
Rumney 7 E2
Runcorn 19 F1
Runwell 11 D1
Rush Green 51 G3
Rushall *W.Mid.* 20 B4
Rushall *W.Mid.* 52 C1
Rushden 15 F1
Rushmere St. Andrew
17 E2
Rushock 52 A4
Ruskington 22 A2
Ruspidge 14 A3
Rustington 10 A4
Rutherglen 33 F2
Ruthin 19 D2
Ruyton-XI-Towns
19 F3
Ryde 9 E3
Rye 11 E3
Rye Park 51 E1
Ryhall 21 F3
Ryton-on-Dunsmore 53 F4

S

Sacriston 30 C2
Saddell 32 C3
Saffron Walden 16 B2
Saham Toney 23 D4
Saighdinis 46 B1

St. Abbs 35 E1
St. Agnes 3 E3
St. Albans 16 A3
St. Albans 50 C1
St. Andrews 39 E4
St. Asaph (Llanelwy)
19 D1
St. Athan 7 D2
St. Austell 4 A3
St. Bees 29 D3
St. Briavels 14 A3
St. Brides Major 7 D2
St. Buryan 3 D4
St. Clears 12 A4
St. Columb Major 3 F2
St. Combs 43 F2
St. Cyrus 39 F2
St. David's 12 A1
St. Day 3 E3
St. Dennis 3 F2
St. Dogmaels 12 A3
St. Endellion 4 A2
St. Enoder 3 F2
St. Fergus 43 F2
St. Fillans 38 A3
St. Germans 4 B3
St. Helens *Mersey.*
25 D4
St. Ishmael 6 B1
St. Ive 4 B2
St. Ives *Cambs.* 16 A1
St. Ives *Cornw.* 3 D3
St. John's Chapel 30 B2
St. John's Town of Dalry
28 C1
St. Just 3 D3
St. Just in Roseland 3 F3
St. Keverne 3 F4
St. Leonards 8 C3
St. Margaret's at Cliffe
11 F2
St. Margaret's Hope
49 E4
St. Martin's 19 E3
St. Mary Bourne 9 D1
St. Mary Cray 51 F5
St. Mary's 49 E3
St. Mary's Bay 11 E3
St. Mawes 3 F3
St. Merryn 3 F2
St. Monans 39 E4
St. Neots 16 A1
St. Osyth 17 E3
St. Paul's Cray 51 F5
St. Peter's 11 F1
St. Stephen 3 F2
St. Stephens *Herts.*
50 C1
St. Teath 4 A2
Salcombe 4 C3
Sale 25 E4
Salen *Arg. & B.* 36 C3
Salen *High.* 37 D2
Salford *Gt.Man.* 25 E4
Salfords 10 B2
Salhouse 23 E3
Saline 34 A1
Salisbury 8 C2
Salsburgh 34 A2
Salt Hill 50 A4
Saltash 4 B2
Saltburn-by-the-Sea 31 E3
Saltcoats 33 E3
Saltdean 10 B4
Saltford 8 A1
Saltley 52 C3
Saltney 19 E2

Sanaigmore 32 A1
Sandbach 20 A1
Sanderstead 51 E5
Sandgarth 49 E3
Sandhead 28 A2
Sandhurst 9 F1
Sandiacre 21 D2
Sandness 48 A3
Sandown 9 E4
Sandplace 4 B3
Sandridge 16 A3
Sandsend 31 F3
Sandwich 11 F2
Sandwick 48 B4
Sandy 16 A2
Sandygate 24 B2
Sanquhar 34 A4
Sapcote 21 D4
Sarratt 50 B2
Sarre 11 F2
Satley 30 C2
Saundersfoot 6 A1
Sawbridgeworth 16 B3
Sawston 16 B2
Sawtry 16 A1
Saxilby 21 F1
Saxmundham 17 F1
Saxthorpe 23 E3
Scalasaig 36 B4
Scalby 31 F4
Scalloway 48 B3
Scampton 21 F1
Scapa 49 E3
Scarborough 31 F4
Scarcliffe 21 D1
Scarinish 36 A3
Scarisbrick 24 C3
Scleddau 12 B1
Scole 17 E1
Sconser 40 B3
Scorton 30 C4
Scotch Corner 30 C4
Scotter 26 C4
Scotton 30 C4
Scourie 44 A2
Scousburgh 48 B4
Scrabster 45 E1
Scraptoft 21 E3
Scremerston 35 E2
Scunthorpe 26 C3
Seaford 10 C4
Seahouses 35 F3
Seamer *N.Yorks.* 26 C1
Seamill 33 E2
Seascale 29 E4
Seaton *Cumb.* 29 E3
Seaton *Devon* 5 E1
Seaton Delaval 31 D1
Seaton Sluice 31 D1
Seckington 53 E1
Sedbergh 30 A4
Sedgebrook 21 F2
Sedgefield 31 D3
Sedgley 20 B4
Sedgley 52 B2
Seend 8 B1
Seer Green 50 A2
Seghill 31 D1
Seighford 20 B3
Seisdon 52 A2
Selattyn 19 E3
Selby 26 B3
Selkirk 34 C2
Sellafield 29 E4
Sellafirth 48 C1
Sellindge 11 E3

Selly Oak 52 C3
Selsdon 51 E5
Selsey 9 F4
Selston 21 D2
Send 10 A2
Sennen 3 D4
Sennybridge 13 D4
Setter 48 B3
Settle 25 E1
Seven Kings 51 F3
Seven Sisters 7 D1
Sevenoaks 10 C2
Severn Beach 7 F2
Sewardstone 51 E2
Sgiogarstaigh 47 F1
Shackerley 52 A1
Shackerstone 53 F1
Shaftesbury 8 B2
Shalfleet 9 D4
Shalford 10 A2
Shanklin 9 E4
Shap 30 A3
Shareshill 52 B1
Sharpness 14 A3
Shavington 20 A2
Shaw 25 E3
Sheepy Magna 53 F1
Sheepy Parva 53 F1
Sheering 16 B3
Sheerness 11 D1
Sheffield 26 A4
Sheffield City Airport
26 A4
Shefford 16 A2
Shelf 25 F3
Sheldon *W.Mid.* 53 D3
Shelf 25 F3
Shelfield 52 C1
Shelley *Essex* 51 G1
Shellow Bowells 51 H1
Shenfield 51 H2
Shenley 50 C1
Shenleybury 50 C1
Shenstone *Worcs.*
52 A4
Shenstone *Staffs.* 20 C3
Shenstone *Staffs.* 53 D1
Shenstone Woodend
53 D1
Shenton 53 F1
Shepley 25 F3
Shepperton 10 A2
Shepperton 50 B5
Shepshed 21 D3
Shepton Mallet 8 A2
Sherborne 8 A3
Sherborne St. John 9 E1
Sherburn 31 D2
Sherburn in Elmet 26 A2
Shere 10 A2
Sheriff Hutton 26 B1
Sheriffhales 20 A3
Sheringham 23 E2
Sherston 14 B4
Shevington 25 D3
Shiel Bridge 41 D4
Shieldaig 40 C2
Shifnal 20 A3
Shilbottle 35 F4
Shildon 30 C3
Shinfield 9 F1
Shinness Lodge 44 C3
Shiplake 15 E4
Shipley *Shrop.* 52 A2
Shipley *W.Yorks.* 25 F2
Shipston on Stour
14 C2
Shipton *N.Yorks.* 26 B1

Shipton *Shrop.* 20 A4
Shipton-under
Wychwood 14 C3
Shirebrook 21 D1
Shiremoor 31 D1
Shirenewton 7 F1
Shirland 21 D1
Shirley *Gt.Lon.* 51 E5
Shirley *W.Mid.* 53 D4
Shoeburyness 11 E1
Shooter's Hill 51 F4
Shoreditch 51 E3
Shoreham *Kent* 10 C2
Shoreham *Kent* 51 G5
Shoreham-by-Sea 10 B4
Short Heath *W.Mid.*
52 C2
Shotley Gate 17 E2
Shotton *Flints.* 19 E2
Shotts 34 A2
Shrawley 52 A5
Shrewley 53 E5
Shrewsbury 13 F1
Shrewton 8 C2
Shrivenham 14 C4
Shustoke 53 E2
Shuttington 53 E1
Siabost 47 E1
Sible Hedingham 16 C2
Sibsey 22 B2
Sibson *Leics.* 53 F1
Sidbury 5 E1
Sidcup 10 C1
Sidcup 51 F4
Sidemoor 52 B4
Sidford 5 E1
Sidley 11 D4
Sidmouth 5 E1
Sigglesthorne 27 D2
Sileby 21 D3
Silloth 29 E2
Silsden 25 F2
Silverdale *Lancs.* 24 C1
Silverstone 15 E2
Silverton 5 D1
Simonsbath 6 C3
Singlewell or Ifield
51 H4
Sipson 50 B4
Sittingbourne 11 D2
Siulaisiadar 47 F2
Skaill (East Coast) *Ork.*
49 F3
Skaill (West Coast) *Ork.*
49 D3
Skaw 48 C2
Skegness 22 B1
Skelmersdale 24 C3
Skelmorlie 33 E2
Skelton 31 E3
Skelwick 49 E2
Skenfrith 13 F4
Skerray 44 C1
Skipness 32 C2
Skipsea 27 D2
Skipton 25 E2
Slade Green 51 G4
Slaidburn 25 D2
Slaithwaite 25 F3
Slamannan 34 A1
Sleaford 21 F2
Sledmere 26 C1
Sleights 31 F3
Sligachan 40 B3
Slinfold 10 A3
Slough 10 A1

Slough 50 A4
Smailholm 35 D3
Smalley 21 D2
Smeeth 11 E3
Smethwick 20 B4
Smethwick 52 C3
Smug Oak 50 C1
Snainton 26 C1
Snaith 26 B3
Snarestone 53 F1
Snettisham 22 C3
Snitterfield 14 C1
Snodland 11 D2
Soham 16 B1
Solas 46 B1
Sole Street *Kent* 51 H5
Solihull 20 C4
Solihull 53 D4
Solihull Lodge 52 C4
Solva 12 A1
Somercotes 21 D2
Somersham 16 B1
Somerton 7 F4
Sompting 10 B4
Sonning Common 15 E4
Sorbie 28 B2
Sorisdale 36 B2
Sorn 33 F3
South Anston 26 B4
South Bank 31 E3
South Beddington 50 D5
South Benfleet 11 D1
South Brent 4 C2
South Cave 26 C3
South Chard 5 F1
South Darenth 51 G5
South Harting 9 F2
South Hetton 31 D2
South Hornchurch 51 G3
South Kelsey 27 D4
South Kirkby 26 A3
South Leverton 26 C4
South Lopham 17 D1
South Mimms 50 D1
South Molton 6 C4
South Normanton 21 D1
South Norwood 51 E5
South Ockendon 10 C1
South Ockendon 51 G3
South Oxhey 10 A1
South Oxhey 50 C2
South Petherton 7 F4
South Queensferry
34 B1
South Shields 31 D1
South Skirlaugh 27 D2
South Street *Kent*
51 H5
South Weald 51 G2
South Woodham Ferrers
16 C4
South Wootton 22 C3
South Yardley 53 D3
Southall 50 C4
Southam 15 D1
Southampton 9 E3
Southampton
International Airport
9 D3
Southborough 10 C3
Southbourne *W.Suss.* 9 F3
Southdean 35 D4
Southend *Arg. & B.* 32 C4
Southend-on-Sea 11 D1
Southery 22 C4
Southfleet 51 H4
Southgate *Gt.Lon.* 10 B1

Southgate *Gt.Lon.*
50 D2
Southminster 17 D4
Southport 24 C3
Southwark 51 E4
Southwick *Wilts.* 8 B1
Southwold 17 F1
Sowerby 26 A1
Sowerby Bridge 25 F3
Spalding 22 A3
Spean Bridge 37 F1
Speen 9 D1
Spennymoor 31 D3
Spey Bay 42 C2
Spilsby 22 B1
Spinningdale 42 A1
Spital *W. & M.* 50 A4
Spitalbrook 51 E1
Spittal 45 E2
Spittal of Glenshee
38 C2
Spixworth 23 E3
Spofforth 26 A2
Springfield *W.Mid.*
52 C3
Springholm 29 D1
Springside 33 E3
Sproatley 27 D2
Sprowston 23 E3
Sproxton 26 B1
Stadhampton 15 E3
Stadhlaigearraidh 46 A2
Staffin 40 B2
Stafford 20 B3
Staindrop 30 C3
Staines 10 A1
Staines 50 B4
Stainforth *N.Yorks.*
25 E1
Stainforth *S.Yorks.*
26 B3
Staintondale 31 F4
Stalbridge 8 B3
Stalham 23 F3
Stalling Busk 30 B4
Stalybridge 25 E4
Stamford 21 F3
Stamfordham 30 C1
Standeford 52 B1
Standish 25 D3
Standon 16 B3
Stane 34 A2
Stanford Rivers 51 G1
Stanford-le-Hope 11 D1
Stanhoe 22 C2
Stanhope 30 B2
Stanley *Dur.* 30 C2
Stanley *P. & K.* 38 C3
Stanley *W.Yorks.* 26 A3
Stanmore *Gt.Lon.* 50 C2
Stannington *Nhumb.*
30 C1
Stansted 51 H5
Stansted Airport 16 B3
Stansted Mountfitchet
16 B3
Stanton 17 D1
Stanway 17 D3
Stanwell 50 B4
Stanwell Moor 50 B4
Stapleford *Notts.* 21 D2
Stapleford Abbotts 51 F2
Stapleford Tawney 51 G2
Staplehurst 11 D2
Starcross 5 D2
Startforth 30 C3

Staunton 14 A2
Staveley 21 D1
Staxton 27 D1
Steeple Claydon 15 E2
Steeton 25 F2
Stenhousemuir 34 A1
Stenness 48 A2
Stenton 35 D1
Stepney 51 E3
Stevenage 16 A3
Stevenston 33 E3
Stewarton 33 E2
Steyning 10 B4
Stibb Cross 6 B4
Stichill 35 D3
Stickney 22 B2
Stillington *N.Yorks.*
26 B1
Stilton 22 A4
Stirchley *W.Mid.* 52 C3
Stirling 34 A1
Stivichall 53 F4
Stobo 34 B3
Stock 16 C4
Stockbridge 9 D2
Stockingford 53 F2
Stockport 25 E4
Stocksbridge 26 A4
Stocksfield 30 C2
Stockton Heath 19 F1
Stockton-on-Tees 31 D3
Stoer 44 A3
Stoke *W.Mid.* 53 F4
Stoke Albany 21 E4
Stoke Ash 17 E1
Stoke Golding 53 F2
Stoke Holy Cross 23 E4
Stoke Mandeville 15 F3
Stoke Newington 51 E3
Stoke Poges 10 A1
Stoke Poges 50 A3
Stoke Prior *Worcs.*
14 B1
Stoke Prior *Worcs.*
52 B5
Stoke-by-Nayland 17 D2
Stoke-on-Trent 20 B2
Stokenchurch 15 E4
Stokenham 5 D3
Stokesay 13 F2
Stokesley 31 E4
Stondon Massey 51 G1
Stone *Glos.* 14 A4
Stone *Worcs.* 52 A4
Stone *Kent* 10 C1
Stone *Kent* 51 G4
Stone *Staffs.* 20 B2
Stonebridge *Warks.*
53 E3
Stonehaven 39 F1
Stonehouse *Glos.* 14 A3
Stonehouse *S.Lan.*
34 A2
Stoneleigh 53 F4
Stoneykirk 28 A2
Stonnall 52 C1
Stony Stratford 15 E2
Stornoway 47 F2
Storrington 10 A4
Stotfold 16 A2
Stourbridge 20 B4
Stourbridge 52 A3
Stourport-on-Severn 14 A1
Stourport-on-Severn 52 A4
Stourton *Staffs.* 52 A3
Stow 34 C2
Stow-on-the-Wold 14 C2

Stowmarket 17 D2
Strachan 39 E1
Strachur 37 E4
Stradbroke 17 E1
Stradishall 16 C2
Stradsett 22 C4
Straloch 38 C2
Stranraer 28 A2
Stratford-upon-Avon
14 C1
Strathaven 33 F2
Strathblane 33 F1
Strathdon 42 C4
Strathmiglo 38 C4
Strathpeffer 41 F2
Strathy 45 D1
Strathyre 38 A4
Stratton 4 B1
Stratton St. Margaret
14 C4
Streatham 50 D4
Streatley 15 E4
Street 7 F4
Streetly 52 C2
Strensall 26 B1
Stretford 25 E4
Stretham 16 B1
Stretton (Burton upon
Trent) *Staffs.* 20 C3
Strichen 43 F2
Stromeferry 40 C3
Stromness 49 D3
Stronachlachar 37 F4
Strone 33 E1
Strontian 37 D2
Stroud 14 B3
Stuartfield 43 F3
Studley *Warks.* 14 C1
Studley *Warks.* 52 C5
Studley Common 52 C5
Sturminster Newton
8 B3
Sturry 11 E2
Sturton le Steeple 26 C4
Sudbury *Derbys.* 20 C2
Sudbury *Gt.Lon.* 50 C3
Sudbury *Suff.* 17 D2
Sully 7 E2
Sumburgh 48 B4
Summer Bridge 25 F1
Sunbury 10 A1
Sunbury 50 C5
Sunderland 31 D2
Sunningdale 50 A5
Sunninghill 9 F1
Sunninghill 50 A5
Surbiton 50 C5
Surfleet 22 A3
Sutterton 22 A3
Sutton *Gt.Lon.* 50 D5
Sutton (Ely) *Cambs.*
16 B1
Sutton at Hone 51 G4
Sutton Bridge 22 B3
Sutton Coldfield 20 C4
Sutton Coldfield 53 D2
Sutton Courtenay 15 D4
Sutton in Ashfield 21 D1
Sutton on Trent 21 E1
Sutton Valence 11 D2
Sutton-on-the-Forest
26 B1
Swadlincote 20 C3
Swaffham 22 C4
Swanage 8 C4
Swanland 26 C3
Swanley 10 C2

Swanley 51 G5
Swanscombe 10 C1
Swanscombe 51 H4
Swansea 6 C1
Swanton Morley 23 D3
Sway 9 D3
Swindon *Staffs.* 52 A2
Swindon *Swin.* 14 C4
Swindon Village 14 B2
Swinefleet 26 C3
Swinton *Gt.Man.* 25 E4
Swinton *Sc.Bord.* 35 E2
Swinton *S.Yorks.* 26 A4
Sydenham *Gt.Lon.*
51 E4
Symbister 48 C3
Symington *S.Ayr.* 33 E3
Symington *S.Lan.* 34 A3
Synod Inn 12 B3
Syre 44 C2
Syston 21 E3
Sytchampton 52 A5

T

Tabost 47 F1
Tadcaster 26 A2
Tadley 9 E1
Taffs Well 7 E2
Tain 42 A1
Takeley 16 B3
Talgarreg 12 B3
Talgarth 13 E4
Taliesin 12 C2
Talisker 40 A3
Talladale 41 D2
Tamworth 20 C3
Tamworth 53 E1
Tannadice 39 E2
Tansley 21 D1
Tanworth in Arden
53 D4
Taobh Tuath 47 D3
Tarbert (Jura) *Arg. & B.*
32 B1
Tarbert (Kintyre)
Arg. & B. 32 C2
Tarbet 37 F4
Tarbolton 33 F3
Tardebigge 52 B5
Tarfside 39 E1
Tarleton 24 C3
Tarporley 19 F2
Tarrel 42 B1
Tarves 43 E3
Tarvin 19 F2
Tattershall 22 A2
Taunton 7 E4
Taverham 23 E3
Tavistock 4 C2
Tayinloan 32 C2
Taynuilt 37 E3
Tayport 39 D3
Tayvallich 32 C1
Teangue 40 C4
Tebay 30 A4
Teddington *Gt.Lon.* 50 C4
Tees-side International
Airport 31 D3
Teignmouth 5 D2
Telford 20 A3
Temple Bar 12 B3
Temple Sowerby 30 A3
Templeton 6 A1
Tenbury Wells 14 A1
Tenby 6 A1
Tenterden 11 D3

Terrington 26 B1
Terrington St. Clement
22 B3
Tetbury 14 B4
Tetford 22 A1
Tetney 27 E4
Tettenhall 52 A1
Tettenhall Wood 52 A2
Teviothead 34 C4
Tewkesbury 14 B2
Teynham 11 E2
Thame 15 E3
Thames Ditton 50 C5
Thamesmead 51 F3
Thatcham 9 E1
Thaxted 16 C3
The Bratch 52 A2
The Burf 52 A5
The Mumbles 6 C2
The Stocks 11 D3
The Wrythe 50 D5
Theale 15 E4
Thetford 17 D1
Theydon Bois 51 F2
Thirsk 26 A1
Thong 51 H4
Thornaby-on-Tees 31 D3
Thornbury 14 A4
Thorne 26 B3
Thornes 52 C1
Thorney *Bucks.* 50 B4
Thorney *Peter.* 22 A4
Thorngumbald 27 D3
Thornhill *D. & G.* 34 A4
Thornhill *Stir.* 38 A4
Thornley 31 D2
Thornton *Fife* 39 D4
Thornton *Lancs.* 24 C2
Thornton *Mersey.* 24 C4
Thornton Dale 27 D1
Thornwood Common
51 F1
Thorpe *Surr.* 50 B5
Thorpe Constantine
53 E1
Thorpe Market 23 E2
Thorpe on the Hill *Lincs.*
21 F1
Thorpe St. Andrew 23 E4
Thorpe-le-Soken 17 E3
Thorpeness 17 F1
Thrapston 21 F4
Threlkeld 29 F3
Threshers Bush 51 F1
Threshfield 25 E1
Thropton 35 E4
Thrumster 45 F2
Thrupp 14 B3
Thrybergh 26 A4
Thundersley 11 D1
Thurcroft 26 A4
Thurlby 22 A3
Thurmaston 21 E3
Thurnscoe 26 A4
Thursby 29 F2
Thurso 45 E1
Thurton 23 E4
Thwaite 30 B4
Tibbermore 38 C3
Tibshelf 21 D1
Ticehurst 11 D3
Tickhill 26 B4
Ticknall 21 D3
Tidenham 14 A4
Tideswell 20 C1
Tighnabruaich 33 D1
Tilbury 10 C1

Tilbury 51 H4
Tile Cross 53 D3
Tile Hill 53 E4
Tilehurst 15 E4
Tillicoultry 38 B4
Tillyfourie 43 D4
Tilston 19 F2
Timsbury 8 A1
Timsgearraidh 47 D2
Tingewick 15 E2
Tingwall 49 E3
Tintagel 4 A1
Tintern Parva 7 F1
Tipton 52 B2
Tiptree 17 D3
Tisbury 8 B2
Tiverton 7 D4
Toab 48 B4
Tobermory 36 C2
Toberonochy 37 D4
Toddington Beds. 15 F2
Toddington Glos. 14 B2
Toft 48 B2
Togston 35 F4
Tolastadh a'Chaolais 47 E2
Tolastadh Ur 47 F1
Toll of Birness 43 F3
Tollesbury 17 D3
Tolleshunt D'Arcy 17 D3
Tolworth 50 C5
Tomatin 42 A3
Tomich 42 A2
Tomintoul 42 C4
Tomnavoulin 42 C3
Tonbridge 10 C2
Tongland 28 C2
Tongue 44 C2
Tonna 6 C1
Tonyrefail 7 D2
Toot Hill 51 G1
Topcliffe 26 A1
Topsham 5 D1
Tore 41 F2
Tormore 32 C3
Torphichen 34 A1
Torphins 43 D4
Torpoint 4 B3
Torquay 5 D2
Torrance 33 F1
Torridon 41 D2
Torrin 40 B4
Torthorwald 29 E1
Torver 29 F4
Toscaig 40 C3
Tosside 25 E2
Totland 9 D4
Totnes 5 D2
Tottenham 51 E2
Totteridge 50 D2
Tottington 25 E3
Totton 9 D3
Tow Law 30 C2
Towcester 15 E2
Tower Hamlets 51 E3
Town Yetholm 35 E3
Townhead of Greenlaw
  29 D1
Towyn 19 D1
Tranent 34 C1
Trawsfynydd 18 C3
Trecastle 13 D4
Tredegar 7 E1
Tredington 14 C2
Treeton 26 A4
Trefaldwyn
  (Montgomery) 13 E1

Trefeglwys 13 D2
Trefriw 18 C2
Trefynwy (Monmouth)
  7 F1
Tregaron 12 C3
Tregony 3 F3
Tregynon 13 E1
Treharris 7 E1
Treherbert 7 D1
Trelech 12 A4
Trelleck 7 F1
Tremadog 18 B3
Trenance 3 F2
Treorchy 7 D1
Trescott 52 A2
Tressait 38 B2
Tretower 13 E4
Trimdon 31 D3
Trimsaran 6 B1
Tring 15 F3
Trinity 39 E2
Trochry 38 C3
Troedyrhiw 7 E1
Troon 33 E3
Troutbeck 29 F4
Troutbeck Bridge 29 F4
Trowbridge 8 B1
Trumpington 16 B2
Truro 3 F3
Trysull 52 A2
Tudweiliog 18 A3
Tummel Bridge 38 B2
Tunga 47 F2
Tunstall Suff. 17 F2
Turnberry 33 E4
Turner's Green 53 D4
Turners Hill 10 B3
Turnford 51 E1
Turriff 43 E2
Tutbury 20 C3
Tutnall 52 B4
Tutshill 7 F1
Tuxford 21 E1
Twatt 49 D3
Twechar 33 F1
Tweedmouth 35 E2
Tweedsmuir 34 B3
Twickenham 50 C4
Two Gates 53 E1
Twycross 53 F1
Twyford W'ham 15 E4
Twyford Hants. 9 E2
Twynholm 28 C2
Twynning 14 B2
Tyburn 53 D2
Tye Common 51 H2
Tylers Green Essex 51 G1
Tyndrum 37 F3
Tynemouth 31 D1
Tythegston 7 D2
Tywardreath 4 A3
Tywyn 12 C1

U
Uachdar 46 B2
Uckfield 10 C3
Uddingston 33 F2
Uddington 34 A3
Uffculme 7 E4
Ufton 53 F5
Uig 40 B2
Ulbster 45 F2
Ulceby 27 D3
Ulgham 35 F4
Ullapool 41 D1
Ullenhall 53 D5

Ulleskelf 26 B2
Ulpha 29 E4
Ulsta 48 B2
Ulverston 24 C1
Umberleigh 6 C4
Unapool 44 B2
Undy 7 F2
Unstone 21 D1
Up Holland 25 D4
Upavon 8 C1
Uphampton 52 A5
Uplyme 5 F1
Upminster 51 G3
Upper Aston 52 A2
Upper Catshill 52 B4
Upper Clatford 9 D2
Upper Eastern Green 53 E3
Upper Gornal 52 B2
Upper Halliford 50 B5
Upper Heyford 15 D2
Upper Knockando 42 C3
Upper Ludstone 52 A2
Upper Mitton 52 A4
Upper Norwood 51 E4
Upper Stoke 53 F3
Upper Tean 20 B2
Upper Tooting 50 D4
Uppingham 21 F4
Upshire 51 F1
Upton Slo. 50 A4
Upton Ches. 19 F2
Upton Dorset 8 C3
Upton St. Leonards 14 B3
Upton upon Severn 14 B2
Upton Warren 52 B5
Urafirth 48 B2
Urmston 25 D4
Ushaw Moor 30 C2
Usk 7 F1
Uttoxeter 20 C2
Uxbridge 10 A1
Uxbridge 50 B3
Uyeasound 48 C1

V
Valley 18 A1
Valsgarth 48 C1
Veensgarth 48 B3
Ventnor 9 E4
Verwood 8 C3
Vickerstown 24 B1
Vidlin 48 C2
Viewpark 33 F2
Vigo 52 C1
Vigo Village 51 H5
Virginia Water 10 A2
Virginia Water 50 A5
Voe 48 B2

W
Waddesdon 15 E3
Waddington 21 F1
Wadebridge 4 A2
Wadhurst 10 C3
Wainfleet All Saints 22 B2
Wainhouse Corner 4 A1
Wakefield 26 A3
Walberswick 17 F1
Walderslade 11 D2
Wales 26 A4
Walkwood 52 C5
Wall Staffs. 53 D1
Wall Heath 52 A3
Wallasey 19 E1
Wallingford 15 E4

Wallington Gt.Lon. 50 D5
Walls 48 B3
Wallsend 31 D1
Walmer 11 F2
Walmley 53 D2
Walsall 20 B4
Walsall 52 C2
Walsall Wood 52 C1
Walsgrave on Sowe 53 F3
Waltham 27 D4
Waltham Abbey 16 B4
Waltham Abbey 51 E1
Waltham Forest 51 E2
Waltham on the Wolds
  21 E3
Walthamstow 51 E3
Walton on the Naze 17 E3
Walton-le-Dale 25 D3
Walton-on-Thames 10 A2
Walton-on-Thames 50 C5
Wandsworth 50 D4
Wanstead 51 F3
Wantage 15 D4
Wappenbury 53 F5
Warboys 16 A1
Warcop 30 A3
Ward End 53 D3
Wardington 15 D2
Ware 16 B3
Wareham 8 B4
Wargrave 15 E4
Wark 30 B1
Warkworth 35 F4
Warley 52 C3
Warlingham 10 B2
Warmington 15 D2
Warminster 8 B1
Warrington 19 F1
Warslow 20 C1
Warsop 21 D1
Warton Warks. 53 E1
Warton (Carnforth)
  Lancs. 24 C1
Warwick 14 C1
Warwick 53 E5
Warwick Bridge 29 F2
Wasbister 49 E2
Washingborough 21 F1
Washington T. & W. 31 D2
Wass 26 B1
Watchet 7 E3
Watchgate 30 A4
Water End Herts. 50 D1
Water Orton 20 C4
Water Orton 53 D2
Waterbeach 16 B1
Waterbeck 29 F1
Waterlooville 9 E3
Waterside Bucks. 50 A1
Watford Herts. 16 A4
Watford Herts. 50 C2
Wath upon Dearne 26 A4
Watlington 15 E4
Watten 45 F2
Watton 23 D4
Watton-at-Stone 16 A3
Wealdstone 50 C3
Weatheroak Hill 52 C4
Weaverham 19 F1
Webheath 52 C5
Weddington 53 F2
Wedmore 7 F3
Wednesbury 20 B4
Wednesbury 52 B2
Wednesfield 52 B1
Weedon Bec 15 E1
Weeford 53 D1

Weem 38 B2
Weldon 21 F4
Welham Green 50 D1
Well Hill 51 F5
Wellesbourne 14 C1
Welling 51 F4
Wellingborough 15 F1
Wellington Tel. & W.
  20 A3
Wellington Som. 7 E4
Wells 7 F3
Wells-next-the-Sea 23 D2
Wellsborough 53 F1
Welney 22 B4
Welshpool 13 E1
Welton Lincs. 21 F1
Welwyn 16 A3
Welwyn Garden City 16 A3
Wem 19 F3
Wembdon 7 E3
Wembley 50 C3
Wemyss Bay 33 E1
Wendens Ambo 16 B2
Wendover 15 F3
Wendron 3 E3
Wennington Gt.Lon. 51 G3
Wensley 30 C4
Wentworth S.Yorks. 26 A4
Weobley 13 F3
Wereham 22 C4
Wergs 52 A1
West Auckland 30 C3
West Bergholt 17 D3
West Bridgford 21 E2
West Bromwich 20 B4
West Bromwich 52 C2
West Byfleet 50 B5
West Calder 34 A2
West Coker 7 F4
West Drayton Gt.Lon.
  50 B4
West End (Bisley) Surr.
  50 A5
West End (Esher) Surr.
  50 C5
West Grinstead 10 B3
West Haddon 15 E1
West Hagley 52 B3
West Ham 51 F3
West Harptree 7 F3
West Heath W.Mid. 52 C4
West Hill 5 E1
West Horndon 51 H3
West Hyde 50 B2
West Kilbride 33 E2
West Kingsdown 51 G5
West Kirby 19 E1
West Knapton 26 C1
West Lavington 8 C1
West Linton 34 B2
West Lulworth 8 B4
West Malling 11 D2
West Meon 9 E2
West Mersea 17 D3
West Molesey 50 C5
West Monkton 7 E4
West Moors 8 C3
West Norwood 51 E4
West Somerton 23 F3
West Tarbert 32 C2
West Thurrock 51 G4
West Tilbury 51 H4
West Wickham Gt.Lon.
  51 E5
West Winch 22 C3
West Wycombe 15 E4
West Yell 48 B2

Westbury 8 B1
Westcott 10 A2
Westerdale 45 E2
Westergate 9 F3
Westerham 10 C2
Westfield 11 D4
Westgate 30 B2
Westhill 43 E4
Westleton 17 F1
Westness 49 E2
Westnewton 29 E2
Weston *Dorset* 8 A4
Weston *Staffs.* 20 B3
Weston Green *Surr.* **50 C5**
Weston under Wetherley 53 F5
Weston-super-Mare 7 F3
Westonzoyland 7 F4
Westruther 35 D2
Westward Ho! 6 B4
Westwood Heath 53 E4
Wetheral 29 F2
Wetherby 26 A2
Weybridge 10 A2
Weybridge 50 B5
Weymouth 8 A4
Whaley Bridge 25 F4
Whalton 30 C1
Whaplode 22 A3
Whauphill 28 B2
Wheatley Hill 31 D2
Wheaton Aston 20 B3
Wheddon Cross 7 D3
Whelpley Hill 50 B1
Wherwell 9 D2
Whickham 30 C2
Whiddon Down 4 C1
Whimple 5 E1
Whiston *S.Yorks.* 26 A4
Whitburn *W.Loth.* 34 A2
Whitby *N.Yorks.* 31 F3
Whitchurch *Bucks.* 15 E3
Whitchurch *Cardiff* 7 E2
Whitchurch *Hants.* 9 E1
Whitchurch *Shrop.* 19 F3
Whitecraig 34 C1
Whitehall 49 F2
Whitehaven 29 D3
Whitehill 9 F2
Whitehills 43 E2
Whiteley Village 50 B5
Whiterashes 43 E4
Whitfield 11 F2
Whithorn 28 B2
Whiting Bay 33 D3
Whitland 12 A4
Whitley Bay 31 D1
Whitlock's End 53 D4

Whitnash 15 D1
Whitnash 53 F5
Whitstable 11 E2
Whittingham 35 E4
Whittington *Shrop.* 19 E3
Whittington (Kinver) Staffs. 52 A3
Whittington (Lichfield) Staffs. 53 D1
Whittlesey 22 A4
Whitworth 25 E3
Wick *High.* 45 F2
Wick *S.Glos.* 14 A4
Wick *V. of Glam.* 7 D2
Wick *W.Suss.* 10 A4
Wickersley 26 A4
Wickford 11 D1
Wickham *Hants.* 9 E3
Wickham Market 17 E2
Wickwar 14 A4
Widecombe in the Moor 4 C2
Widford 16 B3
Widnes 19 F1
Wigan 25 D3
Wigginton Staffs. 53 E1
Wigmore 13 F2
Wigston 21 E4
Wigton 29 F2
Wigtown 28 B2
Wilden Worcs. 52 A4
Wildhill 50 D1
Willaston (Wirral) *Ches.* 19 E1
Willenhall (Coventry) W.Mid. 53 F4
Willenhall (Walsall) W.Mid. 52 B2
Willesden 50 D3
Willingale 51 G1
Willingdon 10 C4
Willingham 16 B1
Willington *Dur.* 30 C3
Willington *Derbys.* 20 C2
Williton 7 E3
Willoughby 22 B1
Wilmington *Kent* 10 C1
Wilmington Kent 51 G4
Wilmslow 25 E4
Wilnecote 53 E1
Wilton *Wilts.* 8 C2
Wimbledon 50 D4
Wimblington 22 B4
Wimborne Minster 8 C3
Wincanton 8 B2
Winchburgh 34 B1
Winchcombe 14 B2
Winchelsea 11 D3

Winchester 9 E2
Winchmore Hill *Gt.Lon.* **51 E2**
Windermere 29 F4
Windlesham 50 A5
Windsor 10 A1
Windsor 50 A4
Windygates 39 D4
Winford 7 F2
Wing 15 F3
Wingate 31 D2
Wingerworth 21 D1
Wingham 11 F2
Winkfield 10 A1
Winkfield 50 A4
Winkleigh 4 C1
Winnersh 9 F1
Winscombe 7 F3
Winsford *Ches.* 19 F2
Winsley 8 B1
Winslow 15 E2
Winston 30 C3
Winterbourne 14 A4
Winterbourne Abbas 8 A4
Winterton 26 C3
Winton 30 B3
Winwick *Cambs.* 16 A1
Wirksworth 20 C2
Wisbech 22 B3
Wishaw *N.Lan.* 34 A2
Wishaw Warks. 53 D2
Wistanstow 13 F2
Wistaston 20 A2
Witham 16 C3
Witheridge 7 D4
Witherley 53 F2
Withernsea 27 E3
Witley 9 F2
Witney 15 D3
Wittering 21 F3
Witton Gilbert 30 C2
Wiveliscombe 7 E4
Wivenhoe 17 D3
Woburn 15 F2
Woburn Sands 15 F2
Woking 10 A2
Wokingham 9 F1
Wold Newton 27 D1
Wollaston *Northants.* 15 F1
Wollaston W.Mid. 52 A3
Wolsingham 30 C2
Wolston 15 D1
Wolverhampton 20 B4
Wolverhampton 52 B2
Wolverley *Worcs.* 20 B4
Wolverley Worcs. 52 A4
Wolverton *M.K.* 15 E2

Wolverton Warks. 53 E5
Wombourne 20 B4
Wombourne 52 A2
Wombwell 26 A4
Wooburn 10 A1
Wood End (Redditch) Warks. 53 E3
Wood End (Tamworth) Warks. 53 E2
Wood Green 51 E2
Wood Hayes 52 B1
Woodborough 21 E2
Woodbridge 17 E2
Woodcote 15 E4
Woodford *Gt.Lon.* **51 F2**
Woodford Bridge 51 F2
Woodford Green 51 F2
Woodgate Worcs. 52 B5
Woodgate W.Mid. 52 B3
Woodhall Spa 22 A1
Woodham Surr. 50 B5
Woodingdean 10 B4
Woodland 30 C3
Woodley 15 E4
Woodmansey 27 D2
Woodplumpton 25 D2
Woodside Brack.F. 50 A4
Woodside Herts. 50 D1
Woodside W.Mid. 52 B3
Woodstock 15 D3
Woodton 23 E4
Woodville 20 C3
Wool 8 B4
Woolacombe 6 B3
Wooler 35 E3
Woolmere Green 52 B5
Woolston *Warr.* 19 F1
Woolwich 51 F4
Wootton 15 F2
Wootton Bassett 14 C4
Wootton Wawen 53 D5
Worcester 14 B1
Worcester Park 50 D5
Wordsley 52 A3
Worfield 20 A4
Workington 29 E3
Worksop 21 E1
Wormit 39 D3
Wormley Herts. 51 E1
Worplesdon 10 A2
Worth 10 B3
Worthing 10 A4
Wotton-under-Edge 14 A4
Woughton on the Green 15 F2

Wragby 22 A1
Wrangle 22 B2
Wraysbury 50 B4
Wrea Green 24 C3
Wrelton 31 F4
Wrexham 19 E2
Wrington 7 F2
Writtle 16 C4
Wrotham Hill 51 H5
Wrotham Park 50 D2
Wroughton 14 C4
Wroxhall 53 E4
Wyberton 22 A2
Wychbold 52 B5
Wye 11 E2
Wylde Green 53 D2
Wylye 8 C2
Wymondham *Leics.* 21 F3
Wymondham *Norf.* 23 E4
Wyre Piddle 14 B2
Wythall 14 C1
Wythall 52 C4

Y

Y Drenewydd (Newtown) *Powys* 13 E2
Yapton 10 A4
Yardley 53 D3
Yarm 31 D3
Yarmouth 9 D4
Yarnton 15 D3
Yarrow 34 C3
Yate 14 A4
Yateley 9 F1
Yatton 7 F2
Yaxley 22 A4
Yeading 50 C3
Yeadon 25 F2
Yealmpton 4 C3
Yeovil 7 F4
Yeovilton 7 F4
Yetts o' Muckhart 38 C4
Yiewsley 50 B4
Ynysddu 7 E1
York 26 B2
Youlgreave 20 C1
Yoxall 20 C3
Yoxford 17 F1
Ysbyty Ystwyth 12 C2
Ystalyfera 6 C1
Ystrad 7 D1
Ystradgynlais 6 C1

Z

Zennor 3 D3

INDEX TO PLACE NAMES OF IRELAND

Abbreviations

Ant.   County Antrim   *Kilk.*   County Kilkenny   *Tyr.*   County Tyrone   *Wexf.*   County
Dub.   County Dublin   *Tipp.*   County Tipperary   *Water.* County Waterford

Aasleagh 56 B3
Abbeyfeale 58 C2
Abbeyleix 60 A3
Achill 56 B2
Adare 58 C1
Annahilt 55 E3
Annalong 55 F4
Antrim 55 E2
Ardara 54 B2
Ardee 55 E4
Ardglass 55 F3
Arklow (An tinbhear Mór)
  60 B3
Armagh 55 E3
Armoy 55 E1
Arvagh 57 E2
Ashbourne 60 B1
Athboy 57 F3
Athenry 57 D4
Athleague 57 D3
Athlone (Baile Átha Luain)
  57 E3
Athy 57 F4
Augher 55 D3
Aughnacloy 55 D3
Aughrim 60 B3
Avoca 60 B3

B
Baillieborough 57 F2
Balbriggan 60 B1
Ballaghaderreen
  57 D2
Ballina 56 C2
Ballinafad 57 D2
Ballinalack 57 E3
Ballinamore 57 E2
Ballinasloe
  (Béal Átha na
  Sluaighe) 57 D4
Ballindine 56 C3
Ballinrobe 56 C3
Ballon 60 A3
Ballybay 57 F2
Ballybofey 54 C2
Ballybrack 58 A3
Ballybunnion 58 B2
Ballycanew 60 B3
Ballycastle *Ant.*
  55 E1
Ballycastle *Mayo*
  54 A3
Ballyclare 55 E2
Ballyconnell 57 E2
Ballycroy 56 B2
Ballydesmond 58 C2
Ballygar 57 D3
Ballygawley 55 D3
Ballygorman 55 D1
Ballyhale 60 A4
Ballyhaunis 57 D3
Ballyheigue 58 B2
Ballyjamesduff 57 F2
Ballykelly 55 D2
Ballylynan 60 A3
Ballymacarberry
  59 E3
Ballymacmague
  59 E2

Ballymacoda 59 E3
Ballymahon 57 E3
Ballymakeery 58 C3
Ballymena 55 E2
Ballymoney 55 E2
Ballymote 57 D2
Ballymurphy 60 A3
Ballynahinch 55 F3
Ballyragget 60 A3
Ballyshannon 54 B3
Ballyvaughan 56 C4
Ballyward 55 E3
Baltinglass 60 B3
Banagher 57 E4
Banbridge 55 E3
Bandon 59 D3
Bangor 55 F3
Bangor Erris 56 B2
Banteer 58 C2
Bantry 58 B4
Belcoo 54 C3
Belderg 56 B1
Belfast 55 F3
Belfast International
  55 E3
Belmullet 56 B2
Beragh 55 D3
Bessbrook 55 E4
Bettystown 60 B1
Birr 57 E4
Blackrock 55 E4
Blackwater 60 B4
Blarney 59 D3
Blessington 60 B2
Bohola 56 C2
Borris 60 A3
Borrisokane 57 D4
Borrisoleigh 59 E1
Boyle 57 D2
Bray (Bré) 60 B2
Broadford 58 C2
Broughshane 55 E2
Bunbeg 54 B2
Bunclody 60 B3
Buncrana 54 C1
Bundoran 54 B3
Burtonport 54 B2
Bushmills 55 E1
Butlers Bridge
  57 F2
Buttevant 59 D2

C
Cahermore 58 B4
Cahir 59 E2
Cahirciveen 58 A3
Callan 60 A4
Cappoquin 59 E2
Carlingford 55 E4
Carlow (Ceatharlach)
  60 A3
Carndonagh 55 D1
Carnlough 55 E2
Carrick-on-Shannon
  57 E2
Carrick-on-Suir
  (Carraig na
  Sivire) 60 A4
Carrickfergus 55 F2

Carrickmacross
  57 F2
Carrigallen 57 E2
Carrigtwohill 59 D3
Carrowdore 55 F3
Carrowkeel 55 D1
Cashel 59 E2
Castlebar (Caisleán an
  Bharraigh)
  56 C2
Castlebellingham
  55 E4
Castleblayney 57 F2
Castlebridge 60 B4
Castlecomer 60 A3
Castleconnell 59 D1
Castlederg 54 C2
Castledermot 60 A3
Castlegregory 58 B2
Castleisland 58 B2
Castlemaine 58 B2
Castlemartyr 59 E3
Castlepollard 57 F3
Castlerea 57 D3
Castletown 57 E4
Castletown Bere
  58 B4
Catherdaniel 58 A3
Cavan 57 F2
Celbridge 60 B2
Charlestown 57 D2
Cheekpoint 60 A4
City of Derry Airport
  55 D2
Clady 54 C2
Clane 60 B2
Clara 57 E4
Clarecastle 58 C1
Claregalway 56 C4
Claremorris 56 C3
Clashmore 59 E3
Claudy 55 D2
Clifden 56 B3
Cliffonoy 54 B3
Cloghan 57 E4
Clogheen 59 E2
Clonakilty 58 C4
Clonbern 57 D3
Clones 57 F2
Clonmel (Cluain Meala)
  59 E2
Clonroche 60 B4
Clonygowan 57 F4
Cloonbannin 58 C2
Clooneagh 57 E2
Cobh (An Cóbh) 59 D3
Coleraine 55 D1
Collooney 57 D2
Comber 55 F3
Cong 56 C3
Cookstown 55 D3
Cootehill 57 F2
Cork (Corcaigh) 59 D3
Cork Airport 59 D3
Corofin 58 C1
Courtmacsherry
  59 D4
Courtown 60 B3
Craanford 60 B3
Craigavon 55 E3

Creeslough 54 C1
Cregganbaun 56 B3
Crookhaven 58 B4
Croom 59 D2
Crossgar 55 F3
Crosshaven 59 D3
Crossmaglen 55 E4
Crumlin 55 E3
Crusheen 58 C1
Cullybackey 55 E2
Cushendall 55 E2
Cushendun 55 E1

D
Delvin 57 F3
Dingle 58 A2
Donaghadee 55 F3
Donaghmore 55 D3
Donegal 54 B3
Dooagh 56 B2
Downpatrick 55 F3
Draperstown 55 D3
Drimoleague 58 C4
Drogheda (Droichead
  Átha) 60 B1
Dromod 57 E2
Dromore *Down*
  55 E3
Dromore *Tyr.* 54 C3
Dromore West 56 C2
Drumfree 54 C1
Drumkeeran 57 D2
Drummin 60 A4
Dublin (Baile Átha Cliath)
  60 B2
Dublin Airport 60 B1
Dún Laoghaire 60 B2
Dunboyne 60 B1
Duncannon 60 A4
Duncormick 60 B4
Dundalk (Dún Dealgan)
  55 E4
Dundonald 55 F3
Dundrum 55 F3
Dungannon 55 D3
Dungarvan *Kilk.*
  60 A3
Dungarvan *Water.*
  59 E3
Dungiven 55 D2
Dungloe 54 B2
Dunlavin 60 A3
Dunleer 55 E4
Dunloy 55 E2
Dunmanway 58 C3
Dunmore 57 D3
Dunmore East
  60 A4
Dunmurry 55 E3
Dunquin 58 A2
Durrow 60 A3

E
Edenderry 57 F4
Edgeworthstown
  57 E3
Eglinton 55 D2
Ennis (Inis) 58 C1

Enniscorthy (Inis
  Córthaidh) 60 B4
Enniskean 58 C3
Enniskerry 60 B2
Enniskillen 54 C3
Ennistymon 58 C1

F
Fermoy 59 D2
Ferns 60 B3
Fethard 59 E2
Fintona 55 D3
Fintown 54 B2
Fivemiletown 55 D3
Foxford 56 C2
Foynes 58 C1
Frenchpark 57 D2
Freshford 60 A3

G
Galbally 59 D2
Galway (Gaillimh)
  56 C4
Garvagh 55 D2
Glenamaddy 57 D3
Glengarriff 58 B3
Glengavlen 57 E2
Glenties 54 B2
Gorey 60 B3
Gort 56 C4
Gortahork 54 B1
Graigue 60 A3
Graiguenamanagh
  60 A3
Granard 57 E3
Grange 59 E3
Greenore 55 E4
Gweedore 54 B2

H
Halfway 59 D3
Headford 56 C3
Holycross 59 E1
Horseleap 57 D3
Hospital 59 D2
Howth 60 B1
Hurler's Cross 58 C1

I
Inch *Kerry* 58 B2
Inch *Wexf.* 60 B3

J
Johnstown 59 E1

K
Kanturk 58 C2
Keady 55 D4
Kells *Kilk.* 60 A4
Kells (Ceanannus Mór)
  Meath 57 F3
Kenmare 58 B3
Kilbeggan 57 E4
Kilcolgan 56 C4

Kilcommon 59 E2
Kilcoole 60 B2
Kilcormac 57 E4
Kilcullen 57 F4
Kildare 57 F4
Kilkee 58 B1
Kilkeel 55 E4
Kilkenny (Cill Chainnigh) 60 A3
Killala 56 C2
Killaloe 59 D1
Killarney (Cill Airne) 58 B3
Killenaule 59 E1
Killimor 57 D4
Killinick 60 B4
Killorglin 58 B3
Killurin 60 B4
Killybegs 54 B3
Kilmacrenan 54 C2
Kilmaine 56 C3
Kilmallock 59 D2
Kilmona 59 D3
Kilmore Quay 60 B4
Kilrea 55 E2
Kilrush 58 B1
Kilteel 60 B2
Kiltimagh 56 C2
Kiltullagh 57 D4
Kingscourt 57 F2
Kinnegad 57 F3
Kinsale 59 D3
Kinvara 56 C4
Kirkcubbin 55 F3
Knock 56 C3
Knock Airport 56 C3
Knockalough 58 C1
Knocktopher 60 A4

L

Lanesborough 57 E3
Larne 55 F2
Lauragh 58 B3
Leap 58 C4
Leighlinbridge 60 A3
Leixlip 60 B2
Letterkenny 54 C2
Lifford 54 C2
Limavady 55 D2
Limerick (Luimneach) 59 D1
Lisbellaw 54 C3

Lisburn 55 E3
Lisdoonvarna 56 C4
Lismore 59 E2
Lisnarrick 54 C3
Lisnaskea 54 C4
Listowel 58 B2
Londonderry (Derry) 55 D2
Longford 57 E3
Loughrea 57 D4
Louisburgh 56 B3
Lucan 60 B2
Lukeswell 60 A4
Lurgan 55 E3

M

Macroom 58 C3
Maghera 55 E2
Magherafelt 55 E2
Malahide 60 B1
Malin More 54 B2
Mallow (Mala) 59 D2
Manorhamilton 54 B3
Markethill 55 E3
May's Corner 55 E3
Middletown 55 D3
Midleton 59 D3
Milestone 59 E1
Milford 54 C2
Millstreet 58 C3
Milltown Malbay 58 C1
Mitchelstown 59 D2
Moate 57 E4
Mohill 57 E2
Moira 55 E3
Monaghan (Muineachán) 57 F2
Monasterevan 57 F4
Moneygall 59 E1
Moneymore 55 E2
Monivea 57 D4
Mount Bellew 57 D3
Mountmellick 57 F4
Mountrath 57 E4
Mountshannon 59 D1
Moville 55 D1
Moyvalley 57 F3
Muine Bheag 60 A3

Mullany's Cross 56 C2
Mullingar (Án Muileann gCearr) 57 F3
Mulrany 56 B2
Murrisk 56 B3
Murroogh 56 C4

N

Naas (An Nás) 60 B2
Navan (An Uaimh) 60 B1
Nenagh (An tAonach) 59 D1
New Ross 60 A4
Newbridge 57 F4
Newcastle Down 55 F4
Newcastle Dub. 60 B2
Newcastle West 58 C2
Newinn 59 E2
Newmarket 58 C2
Newmarket-on-Fergus 58 C1
Newport Mayo 56 B2
Newport Tipp. 59 D1
Newry 55 E3
Newtown 59 D2
Newtownabbey 55 F3
Newtownards 55 F3
Newtownbutler 57 F2
Newtownmountkennedy 60 B2
Newtownstewart 55 D2
Ninemilehouse 59 E2
Nobber 55 D4

O

Oldcastle 57 F3
Omagh 55 D3
Oranmore 56 C4

P

Pallas Green 59 D1
Park 55 D2
Partry 56 C3
Pettigo 54 C3
Pomeroy 55 D3
Pontoon 56 C2
Portadown 55 E3
Portaferry 55 F3
Portarlington 57 F4
Portavogie 55 F3
Portlaoise 57 F4

Portlaw 60 A4
Portmagee 58 A3
Portrane 60 B1
Portrush 55 E1
Portsalon 54 C1
Portstewart 55 D1
Portumna 57 D4
Poulgorm Bridge 58 C3

R

Randalstown 55 E2
Raphoe 54 C2
Rathangan 57 F4
Rathdowney 59 E1
Rathdrum 60 B3
Rathfriland 55 E4
Rathkeale 58 C2
Rathkeevin 59 E2
Rathluirc (Charleville) 59 D2
Rathvilly 60 B3
Recess 56 B3
Ringsend 55 D2
Roscommon 57 D3
Roscrea 59 E1
Ross Carbery 58 C4
Rosslare 60 B4
Rosslare Harbour 60 B4
Rosslea 55 D4
Rush 60 B1

S

Saintfield 55 F3
Schull 58 B4
Shanacrane 58 C3
Shannon Airport 58 C1
Shercock 57 F2
Shillelagh 60 B3
Sion Mills 54 C2
Sixmilebridge 59 D1
Sixmilecross 55 D3
Skerries 60 B1
Skibbereen 58 C4
Slane 60 B1
Sligo (Sligeach) 54 B3
Sneem 58 B3
Strabane 54 C2
Stradbally 57 F4
Strangford 55 F3
Stranorlar 54 C2
Strokestown 57 D3

Swinford 56 C2
Swords 60 B1

T

Taghmon 60 B4
Tallow 59 E3
Tandragee 55 E3
Tarbert 58 C1
Templemore 59 E1
Templetuohy 59 E1
Thomastown 60 A4
Thurles (Durlas) 59 E1
Timolin 57 F4
Tipperary 59 D2
Tower 59 D3
Tralee (Trá Lí) 58 B2
Tramore (Trá Mhór) 60 A4
Trim 57 F3
Tuam 56 C3
Tubbercurry 57 D2
Tulla 59 D1
Tullamore (Tulach Mhór) 57 E4
Tullow 60 A3
Tully 54 C3
Tulsk 57 D3

U

Urlingford 59 E1

V

Virginia 57 F2

W

Warrenpoint 55 E4
Waterford (Port Láirgé) 60 A4
Watergrasshill 59 D3
Wellington Bridge 60 A4
Westport 56 B3
Wexford (Loch Garman) 60 B4
Whitehall 60 A3
Whitehead 55 F2
Wicklow 60 C2

Y

Youghal (Eochaill) 59 E3

Alan

28cm lengths
@ 1700 mm

MOF
sapelle wrap

32 mm

x
32 mm   1¾20 mm
32 mm
20 mm